Whatever happened to the Jesus Lane lot?

D1369133

Whatever happened to the Jesus Lane lot?

Oliver R. Barclay

Inter-Varsity Press

INTER-VARSITY PRESS
Universities and Colleges Christian Fellowship
38 De Montfort Street, Leicester LE1 7GP

© INTER-VARSITY PRESS, LEICESTER, ENGLAND

First edition 1977

ISBN 0 85110 396 0

LIBRARY EDITION 0 85110 624 2

Set in Bembo 11/12
Printed in Great Britain by
Hunt Barnard Printing Ltd.,
Aylesbury, Bucks.

Contents

Preface

'The Jesus Lane lot' were the forerunners and, to a considerable extent, the earliest members of the Cambridge Inter-Collegiate Christian Union. The fact that the CICCU completed the first hundred years of its life in 1977 has given fresh stimulus to recording its story before another generation of its leaders has been taken from us. The story is in any case full of challenge and instruction and worth recording; and it has been possible to consult some people whose memories extend to before 1900 and a large number of those whose memories are still fresh from 1919 onwards.

Acknowledgments are listed at the end of the book. But a special word of thanks is due to J. C. Pollock, who has allowed a completely free use of the material in his book, *A Cambridge Movement*, published in 1953.

It would have been possible to give far more detail and to follow up the subsequent biographies of many more of the members. In this short book (of just under two hundred pages for a hundred years!) the author has tried to pick certain main features that are both characteristic of the story and, he believes, of the greatest interest for our thinkng today.

The repercussions have been and still are world-wide. Without doubt there has been a very remarkable work of God in Cambridge University over a hundred years. There is no special human reason why this should have been so, but God's providence and His astonishing mercy have been fresh year after year to changing generations of very imperfect and fallible students, of whom the author was one. Like nearly everyone else in that category, he received in the CICCU infinitely more than he ever gave. The author has written with a great sense of thankfulness to God for His mercies which endure, not only for a hundred years, but for ever.

Chapter One

Beginnings

The University of Cambridge in the 1870s was a typically Victorian middle-class institution. Outwardly it was religious. College Chapel services (conducted strictly in accordance with the Church of England Prayer Book) were compulsory twice on Sunday and several times during the week. There was great respect for the hierarchy of Church and University. Nearly all the students accepted in general terms that Christianity was true – at least *probably true* – though they were not very inclined to do anything about it. Most students were wealthy and had an assured future of influence and leisure, though there were a number preparing for the Church of England ministry who were sometimes very short of money. If so, they were usually looked down on by the rest. For the majority life was easy-going, sociable, dominated by sport rather than work and, for those who could afford it, there was horse racing with betting at Newmarket, only fifteen miles away. It was all very charming, formally rather religious but in reality thoroughly materialistic. Spiritual ambition did not usually survive the pressure for long and many from evangelical homes were lost from a vital faith and drifted into respectable, harmless, self-centred mediocrity.

The founding of a student-led Christian Union in 1877 was therefore a mildly shocking affair. It seemed to be taking religion too far and to have the mark of disrespect for ordained leadership and duly-constituted authority. Certainly it needed a lot of discussion before it was decided to go ahead, but since no-one regarded it exactly as a historic event, it passed without much comment at the time.

The Cambridge Inter-Collegiate Christian Union (always called CICCU) did not arise fully formed out of nothing, however. By 1877 Cambridge had had a considerable period of evangelical influence. There was still much prejudice against religious 'enthusiasm', but the violent opposition of earlier times had weakened.

Simeon and Milner

In 1780, a hundred years earlier, prejudice had been almost universal. At Oxford and at Cambridge, both strongholds of the Church of England, the fear of Methodist or other Free-Church influence had been extreme. Students' papers were carefully vetted before they were accepted, and those suspected of definite evangelical sympathies were usually eliminated. In 1778 six students had been expelled from St Edmund Hall, Oxford on trumped-up charges when they had been found meeting for Bible study. Others were expelled later for being 'tainted with Methodistical principles' and that University earned a reputation for being, if anything, even more hostile to vital religion than Cambridge. At the time these were the only two Universities in England and, since all students had to agree to the Thirty-nine Articles of the Church of England before admission, Free-Churchmen of principle had to go to Scotland for study until University College, London, was opened in 1828 and Oxford and Cambridge were fully opened to others in 1871.[1] Evangelical[2] religion was virtually unrepresented in the University scene of 1780 by students or 'seniors'.[3]

This stranglehold of a formal religion was broken at Cambridge by two men in a partnership of spiritual and secular influence that was an earnest of things to come. Charles Simeon (1759–1836) came up to King's College from Eton in 1779. He was not specially religious but when, in his first week, he received a notice to say that it was compulsory for all students to attend a Communion Service, he took it very seriously and was plunged into alarm and heart-searching. He felt that 'Satan himself was as fit to attend as I'. He was brought to personal faith and peace in his second term through reading a religious book,[4] but apparently knew of no other converted students or like-minded seniors, though in fact there were a few. In 1782, at the age of 23, he became Vicar of Holy Trinity Church, right in the middle of the University area, and began immediately to preach in a way that was virtually unknown in his day. In the same year he became a Life Fellow of King's College and he continued for fifty-four years with one of the most influential ministries that Britain has ever known. Many were converted under his preaching, but he was mocked and ostracized by the majority. When opposition raged and students were even penalized in exams for 'notorious and obstinate Simeonism', he persevered, through much heartache, and built up a core of evangelical students who came to him for mid-week Bible exposition and 'sermon classes' (for ordinands) as well as attending his Sunday preaching. It was said of him that he had more influence than any Archbishop. Because Fellows of Colleges had to be single, he never married, and he also refused all promotion so that he could continue to exercise his ministry to the University. Perhaps partly because he had no human teachers, he developed a plainly biblical approach. He aimed 'never to speak more or less than I believe to be the mind of the Spirit in the passage I am expounding'. He created a new tradition of biblical preaching and teaching and his 'young men' did the same, in their turn, all over the country.

The opposition seems to us today almost incredible. But at that time it was offensive that a man should be so earnest about religion. That anyone should also so condemn all self-righteousness and rely only on the death of Christ was an insult to Victorian religiosity. Even Isaac Milner, the second man in the partnership, who had played a part in Wilberforce's conversion and became Master of Queens' College in 1788, looked on Simeon with suspicion at first. 'I rigorously scrutinized the character and conduct of Mr Simeon, and for a time entertained some doubt of his sincerity,' he wrote. But he became Simeon's staunch friend. In his rather autocratic manner he dominated his College, allowing evangelical students in when it was extremely difficult for them to get in anywhere else. By 1820, when Milner died, Simeon was beginning to be accepted and the University was more open to evangelicals.

Simeon had described his aim as 'to humble the sinner, to exalt the Saviour, to promote holiness'. But it was only when people actually got round to hearing him preach that they were impressed. He and his followers were an object of ridicule and angry criticism. An attempt was made to beat him up, and to be known as a 'Simeonite' or 'Sim' was a passport to contempt. In 1786 and 1796, however, and several times more after 1809, he preached a series of University Sermons in the University Church of Great St Mary (in the usual course of a rota of preachers) and many who came to mock, or to 'scrape' with their feet and so show their disapproval in the echoing galleries, were silenced and impressed.[5] A famine in the town and in the district around Cambridge took place in 1788 and it was discovered that Simeon had been both an organizer of relief and a generous donor (even then practical Christianity made its mark!). In spite of his eccentric ways and donnish manner the town and University began to respect and love him. When he died in 1836 the shops were closed and about half the University came to pay their last respects. Meanwhile hundreds of young men had gone out from his influence as missionaries or ministers. When he started there was only a handful of evangelical clergy left in the Church of England; when he died it was estimated that nearly one third of the pulpits of the Church of England were in evangelical hands, and the flow of active Christians up to the University began to increase. By contrast Oxford was dominated by non-evangelical influences and was about to become the focus of the High-Church 'Tractarian' movement. Neither University College nor King's College, London (opened 1828 and 1831 respectively) was attractive to evangelicals and the only other English University, Durham, was an unknown quantity. In spite of the still dominant influence of a largely formal Anglicanism, Cambridge was the safest place. Young evangelicals therefore tended to come there, if they went to University at all.

'The Jesus Lane lot'

When Simeon died in 1836 he left no student organization behind him. Indeed such a thing was probably unthinkable in his day. But Holy Trinity Church continued the evangelical tradition and the converts of the new evangelical parishes all over the country came in increasing numbers to Cambridge and attended that Church. In this way they got to know one another to some extent, although compulsory College Chapel allowed only limited attendance at town churches. There were, however, four developments that provided major tributaries for the later mainstream of the CICCU, which was to be formed forty years after Simeon's death.

In 1827, following discussion of a sermon by Simeon (we do not know the verse he was expounding), a group of undergraduates had started the Jesus Lane Sunday School. Jesus Lane was then a poor district of the town, and continuous relays of teachers in this mission were themselves greatly helped and enriched. A vision for outreach to fellow-students had hardly developed – that was supposed to be the responsibility of seniors – but at least 'the Jesus Lane lot' were giving out and learning to express the gospel. Many who later became influential Christian leaders (including B. F. Westcott, the Bible commentator and theologian) taught there and a fellowship of witness grew up around this work. It also helped to start several other small missions to townspeople, especially to children, in and around Cambridge.

In 1847 a Christian first-year student (*i.e.* 'fresher') named Albert Isaacs was visited in his rooms the morning after his arrival by an older Christian and drawn into the work of the Jesus Lane Sunday School on his first Sunday. The two men became friends and in 1848 Isaacs suggested that they should join with others in a definite commitment to pray for one another as they prepared for ordination (the vast majority of the men preparing for ordination in the Church of England at that time went to Oxford or Cambridge). They formed the Cambridge Prayer Union or, more correctly, the 'Cambridge Union for Private Prayer, for Members of the University preparing for the Ministry'. The members agreed to pray for each other for an hour once a month. By 1849 they had one hundred members. They never met together, but they prayed amongst other things for 'the raising up of a devoted ministry' and circulated an annual report to which members contributed. In 1850 this was opened also to men who were already ordained and it fairly quickly became dominated by seniors and ceased to have much influence amongst undergraduates. But it was a beginning and showed what student initiative could do.

In 1858 the Cambridge University Church Missionary Union (CMU) was founded with senior help. This met regularly to pray for missionaries, to hear papers given by seniors and to seek to encourage missionary vocation. It was closely linked with the Church Missionary Society, the largest Church of England Society which had, from its foundation in 1799, been a strong force for evangelical

Christianity at home and abroad, not surprisingly, since Simeon and his friends had had a large part in its origin.

The Daily Prayer Meeting

In 1862 the Daily Prayer Meeting was formed. This was again an undergraduate initiative, based on the experience of two freshers who had had such a meeting at school.[6] The school meeting had at first been suspect; but the headmaster, Dr Howson, had been a teacher at Jesus Lane in his day and he encouraged it, with the result that something of a spiritual renewal took place in the school. Now they called for advice from the most evangelical of the Cambridge seniors, including the then Vicar of Holy Trinity Church, but they met with nothing but discouragement. The seniors feared 'excitement'. Did the students not already have 'sufficient means of Grace and perfect Liturgies'? 'Such efforts', they were also told, 'are inconsistent with your present position as undergraduates . . . Assuming the propriety of the movement, *you* are not called upon to undertake it.' One of them therefore consulted Dr Howson again and the other consulted a home Vicar, the famous C. J. Vaughan, who it so happened had also been a Jesus Lane Sunday School teacher. Both of them encouraged the students to proceed and in the teeth of senior disapproval they went ahead 'in fear and trembling'. Twenty men were at the first meeting in a crowded room behind a bookshop in 29 Trinity Street. Opposition was strong. 'Our prayer-meeting', they wrote six months later, 'has met with the disapproval of many of the most esteemed men in our University.' Ordinary undergraduates, including the sons of some distinguished evangelical leaders, called it 'ridiculous', 'awful bosh'. There were never more than thirty present at first. It lasted only half an hour and consisted of two similar sessions, each containing a hymn and a Scripture reading followed by prayer. The informality of men coming dressed for sports seemed eccentric to some observers.

It was an exclusively male meeting and continued to be so until the 1940s.[7]

The leaders of the DPM, as it was always called, began to organize a meeting with a speaker once a term and this was frequently evangelistic in aim. Some of the students were earnest personal evangelists. 'You must give your whole heart to Jesus,' one of them wrote to a friend. 'Keep nothing back. Remember He gave up all for us.' Nevertheless most of the work was done by men who had been convinced Christians already when they came up as students. The DPM shared its premises and its membership with the larger Church Missionary Union. It drew up to 100 on Sundays, and the CMU had 226 on their books in 1875 (the University then had about 2,000 members). The fruits of the ministries of Simeon's young men were beginning to be felt increasingly in the parishes and there were more earnest Christians among the men coming up than ever before. Victorian middle-class home life was deeply influenced by evangelical Christianity. At about this time, however, a new factor entered the Cambridge scene.

Student outreach

In 1871 by Act of Parliament all religious tests were removed from Oxford, Cambridge and Durham. Only when this overwhelming influence of the Church of England was weakened did Free-Church families begin to send their sons in any number to the University. The Free-Churchmen were inclined, of course, to be at least independent of the ordained Church of England University hierarchy. It is not certain how big a part this mixture of a fresh tradition played, but in Cambridge the influx of men of Brethren background[8] was strong by 1880, and by 1886 offensively strong to some of the Anglicans in the CICCU. Robert Armitage resigned from the CICCU Committee then because he felt the Brethren were becoming dominant. Radical Free-Church views were being hotly debated in

1880 under the influence of strong Brethren students such as Granville Waldegrave,[9] though he was chiefly an inspiration for positive evangelism and Bible study. Certainly some of these men injected a fresh and perhaps more reckless concern for evangelism into the more stolid Church of England majority. They must have strengthened the insistence on the need for new birth rather than just baptism. By themselves they would have seemed cranks; but the interdenominational mixture they helped to create had a new vigour.

By 1873 an undergraduate, Sir Algernon Coote, could write, 'There was a large number of out and out Christian men – leaders, too, in boating and athletics – whose one aim and prayer was the desire to lead other men to Christ.' In addition there were also some men outstanding in the academic field and by now not a few of the younger teaching staff were Christians of like mind; but in the student world of the day scholarship was not nearly so important as sport when it came to social influence or 'leadership'. In October a small prayer meeting of friends decided that they must do more to win their friends. They booked the largest hall in Cambridge (the large Guildhall seating 1,300) for Sunday 17 November and sent for a well-known lay evangelist, 'Beauty' Blackwood.[10] He was a man with unusual evangelistic gifts, a Cambridge graduate, and the one through whom Coote himself had been converted earlier. A strenuous effort was made to visit every member of the University. 'I do not mean', wrote Coote, 'that a card was put into the man's door and left there, but the one who had undertaken to ask him went until he found him; whatever the consequences might be, whatever the language used might be, he went until he found him.' Constant prayer was made. In the DPM 'Special Requests Book' (a book in which requests for each day were written on one side and any special answers on the other) a much underlined request is 'for a blessing on Mr Blackwood's visit that many may attend the meeting but especially that *souls may be awakened*'. When the day came the place was packed. It was estimated that well over half the undergraduates of the University were there. There was intense interest. The DPM book had 'For an abundant answer' written for praise opposite the original request, and the further request 'that the impression made by Mr Blackwood's visit may not pass but deepen in all our hearts'. It was the beginning of new life for many and an enormous encouragement to the Christians to come out of their fellowship into bolder and more active evangelism.

The previous few years had also seen the impact of the early 'higher life' or 'holiness' movement. This had its excesses, but it awoke many mediocre Christians to new spiritual zeal. Like many 'revival' movements, the experiences involved seem often to have been experiences of new birth for people previously possessed only of the outward form and beliefs of orthodox Christianity. Some over-reacted against their past heritage, feeling that it had been little more than a legalistic creed. There was a turmoil of beliefs, including some unbiblical emphases, but it stirred the rather staid evangelical world and gave a new desire for each to study the Bible for himself and to be fearless in obeying what he found there. This led to the Broadlands Conference of 1874,[11] where many Cambridge men were present, and in 1875 to the Keswick Convention and other similar gatherings 'for the deepening of spiritual life'. The number of really zealous Christians in Cambridge increased.

Blackwood was invited back to Cambridge for a meeting in the autumn of 1874. He wrote to his wife, 'Great Hall nearly filled. About six hundred. Deep attention for one hour . . . daily prayer meeting attended by seventy down-right men – a marvellous sight. Then down to the river to see Boat Race. Great fun. Saw one man who wished me to be hanged. . . . ' In 1875 there was a more ambitious joint Mission to town and gown. But the climax came in 1876 with a visit by Sholto Douglas, who had been one of the founders of the DPM and was now a vicar in Derby. He met with 200 men the night before for an address and prayer, and preached powerfully on the Sunday. But the important thing was that he stayed up for a whole week. No programme had been arranged, but he went round the Colleges encouraging the Christians. The week closed with a breakfast conference at the Hoop Inn in Trinity Street, at which sixty guests discussed 'how best to carry on God's work amongst undergraduates *by undergraduates*' (italics ours). After eleven speeches and much discussion the party broke up at midday. They had been persuaded that more help was needed for the informal fellowships that Douglas had visited in the Colleges. Something must be added to the DPM and CMU if the evangelistic work was to go ahead.

Within a week a meeting of College representatives had been called in a room on staircase D, Whewells Court, Trinity College. There was much discussion of the numerous problems – not least the snobbery of the University that made it hard for the more aristocratic to accept spiritual leadership from their social inferiors. There was the attitude of seniors to be faced. It was decided to meet again and to plan a larger conference.

Finally on 9 March 1877, four months after Sholto Douglas's evangelistic address, the small Guildhall was filled with about 250 men. Coote was in the chair and Sholto Douglas present. The letter signed by the College representatives and inviting all interested to be present described the object as 'to promote prayerful sympathy between those who are seeking the advance of Christ's Kingdom in the University, and a more entire self-consecration to God's service; to give information generally concerning God's work in the various colleges; and to make suggestions as to the best means of carrying on the work'. Twenty years later R. F. Horton, a student from Oxford (and incidentally a Free-Churchman) who was present, described it as follows:

'There comes back to me a sense of rushing life and assured enthusiasm, young men buoyant and even rollicking, overflowing with animal spirits, but still more with the Spirit Divine. I seem to remember some speeches which had the ring of boyish eloquence in them, and the shout of a King in the midst.' Six days later the Committee met to finalize rules of procedure and to draw up a Constitution. The Committee was to consist of one representative of each College group. Each representative would nominate his own successor, who would be approved by the College group, and the Committee would elect the President and the Secretary who between them carried the administrative load.[12] It was quite naturally called the Cambridge Inter-Collegiate Christian Union. 'We determined', writes Coote, 'that every college in Cambridge where an out-and-out Christian man could be found should be represented on the Union, one such man from each College to be on the executive committee – and we found such men in sixteen out of the seventeen colleges in Cambridge.' 'Before many terms had passed,' concludes Coote, 'the seventeenth college had also its representative.'[13]

It would have astonished the spectators if they had been told this body would still be strong a hundred years later, and that its fundamental beliefs and emphasis would be virtually unchanged. They would have been even more surprised to know that it would play a notable part in the spread of evangelical Christianity through the student world and that it would have at least some indirect influence in the churches in almost every country in the world.

Chapter Two

1877 – 1900
University outreach

The CICCU, then, was started in order to maintain and increase the evangelistic momentum that had gathered from the DPM and the other groupings that had preceded it. It arose immediately out of *evangelistic* activity, and the sense of need that that created for some ongoing organization. It was born in a medium of prayer and foreign missionary zeal; but it represented something new. It was the natural over-spill of spiritual life and it stimulated further life by its corporate activity. The witness was by students to fellow-students. They had seen the need for prayer and fellowship, they had expressed their concern for the poor children of Jesus Lane and the heathen in far-away countries. Now they gave their energies also to their own student community in a new way and did so without losing any of the enthusiasm for those older concerns. In fact the subsequent history suggests that this new sense of responsibility for University evangelism served in the long run to enrich and not to impoverish the other concerns and to avoid some of the dangers of a too-introverted fellowship, which threatened at intervals when the evangelistic emphasis grew weak. Today we would say that they were practising the indigen-ous principle of missionary work, which is that the workers should be people who belong to the community that is being evangelized. The CICCU leaders, however, had no sophisticated principles of mission. They just got on with their responsibilities as they became aware of them and the work prospered.

The founding of the CICCU also represented a new confidence. There had been plenty of rather defensive emphasis on the need to take a stand as a Christian in the extremely 'worldly' society of Cambridge. Now they went over to the offensive and in this context the necessary defensive side of their work took its place more effectively. A biography of the times says that 'it was often a great safeguard in times of enticement to harmful worldly pursuits to be able to say, when invited to go to Newmarket races for instance, or elsewhere, "I have my Sunday School boys to visit or cottage meeting to take, or I have to speak in the Open Air".'[14] To say that no doubt needed courage, but the CICCU had now become more direct. They began to seek to win their friends and not merely to defend themselves from 'enticement'.

Once founded, the CICCU did not lose sight of its aims. During most of these first twenty-three years a University Mission, or other special effort, was mounted every two years and many of the famous evangelists of the time were heard. This tradition did not grow overnight and it owed a great deal to the extraordinary events associated with the Moody Mission of 1882.

The Moody Mission

Early in 1882 J. E. K. Studd, the CICCU President, who was also at the same time University Captain of Cricket, proposed that the American evangelists Moody and Sankey should be invited to Cambridge. Moody had visited Britain several times and had been given an extraordinarily effective ministry to all classes of society, though some thought him vulgar. Studd's father had been converted from a totally worldly life through Moody's Mission in London a few years before and the three sons had all been converted through someone associated with Moody who had become a friend of their father's. But Moody was not a university man, not British, and not middle-class. His education was slender, he was not physically attractive, and he was not really an orator. His addresses were homely talks lit up by anecdotes, often with a kind of humour that some felt was a little too popular for a serious occasion. To bring him to Cambridge, to the most critical and perhaps the most hostile audience available, seemed to older advisers to be rash in the extreme. As events proved the older men were right – it was rash. But it was also of God; and the rashness of student enthusiasm – or was it holy boldness? – won the day. Moody agreed to come and in November 1882 he and Sankey (the singer who usually accompanied him) began a joint Mission to town and University – three services for the town and a late evening service for the students each day! Every undergraduate received a personal invitation, posters were everywhere and special meetings of preparation were held. Handley Moule, one of the senior friends of the CICCU and now Principal of the new evangelical theological college in Cambridge, Ridley Hall, wrote in his diary, 'Lord, be Thou really with me in this coming anxious, responsible time.'

Of all ridiculous days, the Mission started on November 5th, Guy Fawkes' day, which was always given over to bonfires, fireworks and clashes with the police. This year it happened to be a Sunday. The first meeting was held in the new, vast, ugly Corn Exchange with poor acoustics and an atmosphere like a political meeting. Seventeen hundred men in academic cap and gown[15] were counted entering the building, 'laughing and talking and rushing for seats near their friends'. They were in festive mood. The choir – seventy undergraduates of courage ('I would not join that lot for £200,' said one man) – sang hymns as the hall filled up and the audience responded with rowdy songs. Others built a pyramid of chairs. A fire-cracker was thrown against the window. When the platform party came in they were welcomed with cheers and jokes. The opening prayer was greeted with 'Hear! Hear!' and the first solo from Sankey with 'Encore'. At this point some of the most rowdy were ejected, but disturbances continued throughout the evening – bursts of laughter, loud talking, shouts of 'Well done' and humorous questions. 'We went meaning to have some fun', said one man next day, 'and, by Jove, we had it!'

Moody, with his broad American accent, had chosen to speak on Daniel, and his one-syllabled pronunciation of 'Dan'l' was a cause of repeated mirth. Nevertheless, through the heckling and disorder, Moody was heard by the majority and his gift of simplicity and clarity (are these usually part of the gift of the evangelist?) subdued some of the rowdy ones. When the Chairman (John Barton, the Vicar of Holy Trinity Church) invited some to stay and pray, nearly 400 stayed. Moody spoke again, still on 'Dan'l'. When he returned to his hotel and took off his dripping collar he is said to have remarked, 'Well, Sankey, I guess I've no hankering after that crowd again.'

As for the CICCU men, 'with heavy hearts we took our way to our respective Colleges'. Studd sat down next day to write to the weekly *Cambridge Review* and put in the DPM 'Special Requests Book' for Monday, 'Special prayer is requested that God would over-rule any disturbance that may take place tonight.' On Monday, however, only a hundred or so were present in the Gymnasium seating five hundred, where the meetings were held for the rest of the week. It was orderly but depressing. Moody preached on the new birth.

Nevertheless the fruits began to appear. Gerald Lander, one of the fast set and one of the Sunday night rowdies, had commented, 'If uneducated men will come and teach the Varsity they deserve to be snubbed.' But on Monday he went to apologize to Moody and stayed for a long talk. He was there again on Monday night, and with so few present

Moody went round afterwards to speak to each one personally. He was superb at personal evangelism. It was reported that five men professed conversion on the Monday. On Tuesday there was little progress.

Wednesday started the most astonishing five days the University had seen. Studd's letter to the *Cambridge Review* appeared that morning. As Captain of Cricket he was respected and his letter therefore carried some weight. He pointed out that the Americans were guests. 'This being the case you may imagine the disgust which I and many others felt when . . . some fifty, or it might have been a hundred, so far forgot themselves and their assumed character as gentlemen' as to create a disturbance. He politely supposed that these members of the University could not have realized the evangelists' position, 'or they would not have treated the guests of some of their fellow undergraduates, who are also visitors to our country, in such a very ungentlemanly way.' After expressing a hope that they would 'come and hear Mr Moody speak and Mr Sankey sing and that by their attention will show how much they regret having so misunderstood the facts of the case', he concluded with a neat suggestion that this would also forestall any criticism that Cambridge men could not behave as well as Oxford men, 'or even as well as those far below them in the social scale.'

On the Wednesday also Moody asked Christian mothers who had come in for the crowded town meeting in the afternoon to stay and pray for the students – 'some mothers' sons'. A hundred and fifty to two hundred stayed for a moving prayer meeting.

The Gymnasium that night was still not full, but the atmosphere was far removed from that of the Sunday. As Moody spoke he could sense that those mothers' prayers would be answered, and at the end of the address he determined to prove it. 'I have not yet held an inquiry meeting for you, gentlemen,' he said, 'but I feel sure many of you are ready and yearning to know Christ. When you are in difficulties over mathematics or classics, you do not hesitate to consult your tutors. Would it be unreasonable for you to bring your soul-trouble to those who may be able to help you? Mr Sankey and I will converse with any who will go up to the empty gallery yonder ... Let us have silent prayer.'

There was a pause. The gallery, normally used as a fencing room, was reached by a steep iron staircase from the centre of the Gymnasium. To reach it a man would have to face his friends and acquaintances; and even if they were supposed to be praying the clatter of the iron steps would open scores of inquisitive eyes. Moody did not want shallow decisions; as he said on another night that week, 'No-one can have really received Christ in his heart if he does not confess Him to his friends, if only by some small action.'

No-one moved. Then 'amidst an awful stillness' a young Trinity man got up, and 'half hiding his face in his gown, bounded up the stairs two at a time'. Soon the stillness was quite gone, as one man followed another up the iron staircase, while the choir sang a further hymn. Mr Moody remarked, 'I never saw the gowns look so well before' and with Sankey and other helpers went up the stair himself. He found fifty-two men in the gallery. Among them was Gerald Lander, the rowdy of Sunday night.

On Thursday the Gymnasium was fuller (still under 500). Graduates of all persuasions began to come as well as undergraduates. Moody preached on sowing and reaping, but Sankey began to have a real influence also. Arthur Benson (son of the Archbishop), who did not himself find peace with God, described it as follows: 'An immense bilious man, with black hair, and eyes surrounded by flaccid, pendent baggy wrinkles came forward with an unctuous gesture, and took his place at a small harmonium, placed so near the front of the platform that it looked as if both player and instrument must inevitably topple over; it was inexpressibly ludicrous to behold. Rolling his eyes in an affected manner he touched a few simple chords, and a marvellous transformation came over the room. In a sweet powerful voice, with an exquisite simplicity combined with irresistible emotion, he sang "There were ninety and nine". The man was transfigured. A deathly hush came over the room, and I felt my eyes fill with tears; his physical repulsiveness slipped from him and left a sincere, impulsive Christian, whose simple music spoke straight to the soul.'

Then Moody took over. 'He had not spoken half a dozen words before I felt as though he and I were alone in the world . . . After a scathing and indignant invective on sin he turned to draw a picture of the hollow, drifting life with feeble, mundane ambitions – utterly selfish, giving no service, making no sacrifice, tasting the moment, gliding feebly down the stream of time to the roaring cataract of death. Every word he said burnt into my soul. He seemed to me to probe the secrets of my innermost heart; to be analysing, as it were, before the Judge of the world, the arid and pitiful constituents of my most secret thought. I did not think I could have heard him out . . . his words fell on me like the stabs of a knife. Then he made a sudden pause, and in a peroration of incredible dignity and pathos he drew us to the feet of a crucified Saviour, showed us the bleeding hand and the dimmed eye, and the infinite heart behind. "Just *accept* Him," he cried; "in a moment, in the twinkling of an eye you may be His – nestling in His arms – with the burden of sin and selfishness resting at His feet." '

On the Friday the gallery up the iron staircase was packed. Over a hundred were counted. Barclay F. Buxton, a recent Cambridge graduate who was present, wrote later, 'There and then the decision was made. Christ came and for fifty and more years has been my Saviour, Shepherd and King.'[16]

The climax came on Sunday 12 November. The University meeting was back in the Corn Exchange seating nearly 2,500. It was crowded. It was reckoned that well over half the undergraduates of Cambridge were present – perhaps 1,800 were there, plus graduates and some townspeople. There was no opposition – only rapt attention. Moody spoke from Luke 2, 'The angel said unto them, Fear not: for behold I bring you good tidings of great joy, for unto you is born a Saviour, which is Christ the Lord.' 'The angels called it good news,' he began. 'It was either such or it was not such. If it is good news you certainly ought to be glad to hear it; if it is not good news, the quicker you find it it out the better, and dismiss the whole subject!' He went on to speak of the resurrection of Christ, of death, sin, judgment and peace through faith in Christ. 'If the God of the Bible is real, then take your stand, and take it boldly. Don't be religious with religious people, and make sport when with scoffers!' His final theme was 'Seek ye *first* the kingdom of God'.

The lasting results

No-one counted the converts, but about two hundred stood on the last night to indicate that they had received blessing during the week. Handley Moule knew of 'scores of true, deep, lasting conversions'. Ridley Hall (the theological college in Cambridge for graduates) suddenly grew in size and two years later Moule could say that all his students were men whose lives had been 'influenced more or less by Moody's Cambridge Mission'. Not a few, including Gerald Lander and some others who had been notably worldly and selfish men, were giving generously to missionary work within a few weeks and went overseas later as missionaries. A religious journalist wrote that there was a 'marked increase in the attendance at the Daily Prayer Meeting . . . a higher tone of spiritual life among the men – greater prayerfulness, greater diligence in study'. Handley Moule started a series of Bible expositions from the Greek text of the New Testament every Sunday after evening sermon and these became a powerful influence for solid Christian growth and the forerunner of the present Saturday night Bible readings. Douglas Hooper, another Mission convert and a former horse-racing enthusiast who had kept his own horse and trap to take him over to Newmarket, became the founder of the Morning Watch Union. He collected his friends to go to Moule's talks and now got them to sign: 'I will endeavour, God helping me, to set aside at least twenty minutes, and if possible one hour, in the early morning for prayer and Bible study, and also a short but uninterrupted time before retiring to rest.' When he left Ridley four years later to go to Africa as a missionary (where, incidentally, his son and grandson followed in due time), his final words to his fellow-students were not, to their surprise, a missionary exhortation, but 'Remember the Morning Watch!'

In 1885 the CICCU started Sunday night meetings in the Alexandra Hall of the YMCA, where students themselves would speak and give their testimonies. The meetings were held here rather than in a church, because the speakers were not ordained. Again there was a shaking of heads among the older men, but student enthusiasm won; and although the main benefit may have been to the speakers, the meetings were not without fruit. Many students really took a stand for Christ when they agreed to speak at this or at the numerous open-air services held in and around Cambridge. This was also for many the start of a call to full-time ministry. In the summer term the Alexandra Hall meetings were transferred to the open air – on the 'Backs' behind Clare and King's.[17] These meetings were partly the result of influence from the Salvation Army and the 'holiness' movements of the time. After running for a number of years in this way, outside speakers were brought in instead of students for the Sunday night meetings, and the regular Sunday evening evangelistic sermons, which have continued in different places up to the present time, were thus established. They were still in the open air (often in the Market Place) during the summer right up to the 1930s, when it was decided that non-Christian friends were really easier to reach through an indoor service. There developed a tradition of working and

29

praying earnestly to get friends along to these services and then talking to them personally afterwards. Perhaps at times one's success or failure in getting a non-Christian friend along became too much a matter of pride or of legalistic duty. But men were brought to hear the gospel and not a few were converted year by year. George Pilkington (later of Uganda) was one of the most noted converts of the Alexandra Hall meetings. In his first term four Christian freshmen in his college had systematically called on all the other fifty-two students in their year until they had obtained a talk on spiritual things with each one. 'Pilks' wrote them off as mad and criticized fiercely those who continued to try to get him to meetings. But once converted he was as zealous for truth as he had been against it and threw himself into pioneering missionary work as soon as he graduated. A brilliant Classical Scholar, he was soon involved in Bible translation.

The holiness debate
The Keswick Convention was only one aspect of a turmoil of teaching about holiness that began to have a powerful influence in Cambridge at this time. In the same year as the start of the Alexandra Hall meetings John Smyth-Pigott, a rather erratic former Cambridge man of 33 who was now an Anglican curate, came back to Cambridge for a further degree. He and some others with him did not think Keswick went far enough. They taught sinless perfection quite explicitly (*i.e.* that Christians should expect to be completely free of sin). In the lively discussion about holiness, Pigott, perhaps because he was older and because he was extreme, began to have a dominant influence over some. Handley Moule and others became alarmed, but the CICCU President, Douglas Hamilton, came under Pigott's spell. Biblical phrases were used in unbiblical ways. Hamilton came to believe that he had arrived at a new state – he was no longer a sinner and now had direct and authoritative

guidance from God on the smallest matters. He had to obey this guidance even when it seemed contrary to Scripture. He seemed more spiritual than others. Such irrational guidance was impressive to some; but leaving the Bible behind led quickly into disregarding its moral commands and the result was a drift into sexual perversion. Moule and Barton (the Vicar of Holy Trinity Church) spent long hours helping men caught up in the excesses. Some were revolted and gave up all faith; others pulled out in time. Hamilton joined the Agapemonites, a minute sect whose views were a compound of genuine spiritual desire with immorality and plain heresy. He left Cambridge and with Pigott joined the 'Abode of Love' at Spaxton in Somerset, where a community built on their astonishing principles of morality existed. In 1902 Pigott claimed that he was the Immortal Messiah.

This was for a few the tragic climax of what had been for a decade or so a deeply earnest striving after holiness. Moule described the period afterwards as a time of 'wonderful life'. More sober leadership took over, though none the less earnest. A series of Moule's 1884 lectures on sanctification had been published in 1885 under the title *Thoughts on Christian Sanctity* and had steadied many. By 1887 the CICCU was set again on a more solidly biblical course. From forty to sixty were at the Sunday early morning Prayer Meetings and 230 or so at the Alexandra Hall.

Open-airs

Open-air work in the villages around Cambridge was a feature of the work of the more energetic. Douglas Thornton (see next chapter) wrote in his diary, 'In the evening off to Trumpington ... Open air at 7.30. Very clear addresses by Compton on love, Monro on holiness, Hibbert Ware on sin in heart, Woods on redemption, I on acceptance. Three boys I had decided for Christ. Tom Barker had some more. Postman convicted.' Or again, 'Open air on green (at Knap-

well) from 7.30 p.m. to 9.30 p.m. . . . . "There is a green hill"
brought tears to many eyes. Woods on "My Saviour". I
had 14 boys who one by one decided in prayer for Christ
and to read their Bibles. An old woman got blest, . . . Back
9 miles in 35 minutes praising God and running into a
Proctor.'[18]

By the 1890s the CICCU was at the height of its influence
and popularity. It took courage to join it whole-heartedly,
and there were not lacking members who held a rather anti-
intellectual outlook – after all, had not Moody been an
unlettered man? But there was a place for all kinds. G. T.
Manley, who in 1893 became Senior Wrangler (*i.e.* the
best student of his year in mathematics), described it as
follows: 'I entered the University with an idea that evil
companions would surround me on every side; a prospect
which at that time filled me rather with pleasurable antici-
pation than alarm. I was disappointed; for in a year I found
myself for the first time believing in Christ as my Saviour.'
Manley in turn befriended an overseas student on his staircase – Jan Smuts the South African. In after years General
Smuts always treasured a Greek New Testament that
Manley had given him, and when he was in Britain on
important national business would sometimes ring up the
obscure country parson that Manley became after his
missionary career. Manley, in fact, was a great stimulant to
serious discussion, and the CICCU included a Religious
Discussion Society to discuss the antagonisms to Christianity
and equip the members to meet them. But the CICCU was
best known for what C. F. Andrews, then an undergraduate,
described later when he was less sympathetic, as the 'open,
ardent courage, the passionate fervour' of their devotion to
Christ. At this time they also received fresh pastoral and
evangelistic help in the founding in 1895 of the Cambridge
Pastorate. Handley Moule was behind the idea and by 1898
there were two ordained men busy full-time with an endless
round of pastoral counselling and personal evangelism.

There was a link with Holy Trinity Church and Ridley Hall, but the Pastorate was essentially an independent ministry to students. For many years it provided tremendous help to the CICCU.

Meanwhile agnosticism was growing and Bertrand Russell was a focus of attention. Those who thought themselves intelligent, as G. M. Trevelyan once remarked, took it more or less for granted that Christianity was discredited. But the task of the CICCU remained basically the same – to win men for Christ. This by the grace of God they did.

Cambridge in the 1890s was still outwardly religious and the CICCU was its dominant spiritual influence. The Anglo-Catholic group revolving round Little St Mary's Church was small though it attracted some, like C. F. Andrews, who found the CICCU too enthusiastic. The College Chapels, although compulsory, were at best dull and 'were going modernist' already in 1892.[19] Many CICCU leaders went into the ministry if they did not go to the mission field. Ridley Hall, presided over by Moule, was a home of true godliness. The Faculty of Divinity, however, was now teaching moderate liberalism. Theodore Woods, who had been converted as a fresher in February 1893 in an outstanding CICCU Mission led by the Rev. George Grubb, became CICCU President for 1894–5. He had a quite unusual personal influence and was an ardent evangelist of impeccable orthodoxy. His theological studies, however, which he started when he went on to Ridley in 1895, unsettled his views of the Bible. Whereas Moule remained always conservative and taught his men to love the Bible, the Faculty taught something different. Woods' biographer writes, 'Like many other young students at that time he moved slowly and steadily towards' a more liberal view of the Bible. 'This was not without pain and struggle; there were discussions with friends that went on far into the night and stirred many deep searchings of heart.' Like many other ardent and simple evangelists he came out of academic theological study a changed man. No-one had prepared him for it. Even Moule, though he had been Professor of Divinity, was not a very satisfactory guide because he did not really answer the problems.[20] No-one knew quite how to deal with liberalism without being swept away, unless they just brushed it aside. In this decade and the next, very few theological students remained orthodox if they worked hard at theology, unless they were the kind of men who were set on learning only what would serve the interests of evangelistic service. The missionary enthusiasts, for instance, remained on the whole much more orthodox than those who stayed at home. This was partly because they were exposed to liberal pressures for a shorter period, but was also a result of being forced to concentrate on the gospel and not having time to drink deeply of the critical spirit. Critical questions seemed irrelevant to most of them.

Chapter Three

1877 – 1900
Missionary outreach

From the start the CICCU members had a lively interest in overseas missionary work. From its founding in 1858 the Church Missionary Union had flourished and the very influential CMS sent its best speakers to Cambridge. Henry Martyn was remembered with honour. But the Moody Mission and its results were dynamite. During 1883 and 1884 the CMS received a considerable number of offers from men who had been helped or converted in the Mission and other offers came later after ordination.

The Cambridge Seven

But in the autumn of 1884 came the 'Cambridge Seven', who not only had an influence throughout Britain but in their turn stirred Cambridge again to its depths. Stanley Smith, the son of a London surgeon, had come up to Cambridge in 1879 a rather insecure and introspective Christian with indifferent health. After one term at Cambridge he came to a deep, personal experience of Christ, largely through the friendship of a fellow-student, Granville Waldegrave (son of the 'evangelical peer' Lord Radstock). 'I decided by God's grace', he wrote, 'to live for and to Him ... Thank God for sending G. W. here.' He grew in confidence (and in physical strength), and became an ardent personal evangelist and also stroke of the Cambridge boat.

He graduated in '82 and started teaching, but increasingly felt called to missionary service and arranged to talk with Hudson Taylor, the leader and founder of the China Inland Mission. C. T. Studd (the brother of J. E. K. Studd) had begun at Cambridge the same year as Smith, but had been playing cricket for the MCC in Australia during Moody's Mission. He had been converted, like his brother, but his faith remained largely lifeless while he was rising to be captain of University cricket in 1883, and probably the best all-round cricketer in Britain from 1881 to 1884. His name was a household word in sporting circles, but he was spiritually a nonentity. 'Instead of telling others of the love of Christ', he wrote, 'I was selfish and kept the knowledge to myself. The result was that gradually my love began to grow cold, and the love of the world began to come in. I spent six years in that unhappy backslidden state.' He was suddenly brought back to reality by the nearly fatal illness of another brother, who in his illness had cared only about the Bible and the Lord Jesus Christ. God 'taught me the same lesson', he wrote. He immediately set to work for Christ, not least amongst his cricketing friends. Smith, whom he had known in Cambridge, helped him to make progress spiritually and in 1884 they both offered to the China Inland Mission and were accepted.

Some details of the other members of the group are of interest. Dixon Hoste, an army officer, had been influenced by his brother, who was at Trinity College, Cambridge with Smith and Studd. He had also been deeply influenced in the Moody Mission. Dixon had never been at Cambridge himself but was in fact the first of the seven to offer to CIM. Montagu Beauchamp was a cousin of Granville Waldegrave and a prominent oarsman. He was in the same year and college as his cousin, C. T. Studd, and his friend Stanley Smith. Stanley Smith and J. E. K. Studd (also at Trinity College) had met to pray for him every day for a whole term because he seemed at best half-hearted as a

Christian. After a while they had their reward and Beauchamp came to a new spiritual experience. Smith could write 'how marvellously changed he is', and together they started a Bible study for members of the College Boat Club. William Cassels, another Cambridge contemporary (but at St John's College) was an old schoolfriend of Stanley Smith's. Finally there were the two Polhill-Turner brothers. Arthur had been converted in the Moody Mission. He soon started in earnest to try to win his brother Cecil, who had graduated a year earlier. They had both been members of the fashionable and idle set, occupied with theatres, dancing, racing and cards. The change in Arthur's interests was dramatic. He was quickly drawn into the fellowship of the CICCU, attended the Daily Prayer Meeting, and became a particular friend of Beauchamp. He made his brother promise to read the Bible every morning and after a year or so Cecil also became a definite Christian.

All of these seven, linked together by bonds of friendship and Cambridge associations, offered to the China Inland Mission and were accepted, although several of them had only recently become personal Christians. When the news broke it caused a sensation. The CIM was not a well-known society and China at that time was a remote and little-known land. That seven such young men should give up their popularity and extremely good prospects at home to go to such a distant and apparently unimportant work was shattering. That they should do so with such gusto and enthusiasm was profoundly challenging to Victorian complacency. Cambridge in particular was deeply moved and crowded meetings were arranged to hear them speak.

Before sailing Smith and Studd ('SP' and 'CT') undertook in 1885 an extensive tour of a number of universities. They were always enthusiastically received and had many deep, personal talks with undergraduates. They had a particularly important impact in Edinburgh, where they were persuaded to return twice more to crowded audiences (up to 2,000 students, 'the largest meeting of students that has ever been held', and a string of quarter-hour evangelistic talks with individuals all next day). On the first visit a crowd of students went to the railway station to see them off on the night train and demanded another speech on the platform. As the station echoed with resounding cheers a porter drily remarked, 'Th're a' meedical students, but th're aff their heeds!' After the final meeting in Edinburgh the room was still full at half-past ten with men asking, 'What must I do to be saved?' Some who had been converted at the first meeting were already helping their friends and when they were turned out of the hall at midnight the work was still going on. They left behind them an undoubted touch of revival. In Leicester they had a profound influence on F. B. Meyer, launching him on his ministry at Melbourne Hall and later in South Africa. They had asked him, 'Have you ever given yourself to Christ, for Christ to fill you?' Their main emphasis was evangelistic rather than missionary, but their evangelistic message was clearly uncompromising. Smith was something of an orator but Studd, who was a poor speaker, often made a bigger impression by his transparent sincerity and earnestness. A Cambridge student commented, 'I saw that we were to take up our cross and follow Christ: that there was to be no compromise however small, that there was to be nothing between us and our Master.'[21]

Smith and Studd were both aged only 23 at the time and spoke as young men to young men with a power that was evidently of God. The effect was dramatic and it was not a short-lived enthusiasm for them or for many of those they influenced. All the 'Seven' carried out a long spell of missionary work. Stanley Smith's son, grandsons and grand-daughters and at least one great-grandson have also been missionaries. But the 'Seven' provided a far more wide-ranging inspiration and a zeal for missionary work that shook the student world and had an influence on the attitude

to missions throughout Britain. The spiritual impact of the
Moody Mission, the many other evangelistic movements
and the growing influence of the Keswick Convention
were given a fresh foreign missions emphasis that was to
last for a long time. Handley Moule had to plead with his
students at Ridley Hall to stay at home!

Continued missionary zeal

The next few years saw this revival of missionary interest
maintained in Cambridge. The Church Missionary Society
alone had thirty-one CICCU men offer in 1886, and as late
as 1893 140 Cambridge men offered to CMS in the one year.
Over the whole period of the existence of the CMS from
1798 to 1880 it had sent out 156 graduates, of whom seventy-
eight were from Cambridge. In the fourteen years 1881–1894
there were 170 graduates, 100 of them from Cambridge.
Over a quarter of all CMS new missionaries from 1882 to
1894 were CICCU men (95 out of 369) and other societies
probably benefited similarly.[22] One quarter of the CMS
new missionaries from this one small community!

In Cambridge itself the missionary interest was strengthened by the formation of 'Missionary Bands' – groups of
undergraduates who met, usually weekly, for missionary
study, prayer and raising of money for a particular missionary or a particular field. Occasionally they had outside
speakers; usually they read papers to one another. These
Bands seem to have included between a half and a third of
the CU membership and did much to consolidate and
develop what the 'Seven' had begun. The call to all-out
Christian discipleship from then onwards almost always
included the challenge to consider seriously the possibility
of missionary service, with all the hazards that that included
in those days.

The evangelistic concern also was not confined to overseas or to Cambridge. A series of joint annual conferences
was held with the OICCU (Oxford Inter-Collegiate

Christian Union), which had been founded in 1881 largely through the constant encouragement of the CICCU. Mutual interest and prayer became stronger. Moody had gone on to Oxford in 1882 after his Mission in Cambridge and the two Christian Unions developed together. Oxford University, however, was less well supplied with evangelical freshers and its official theological leadership was decisively High Church and more hostile than Cambridge to evangelical Christianity. In the early 1900s an Oxford contingent at the Keswick Convention (including Temple Gairdner and J. H. Oldham) wrote a letter to the Convention leaders asking good evangelical families to send their sons to Oxford. The OICCU was never so strong as the CICCU (until the 1960s), but it also produced its notable leaders and missionaries.

R. P. Wilder

The news of the Cambridge Seven was taken over to the USA in the summer of 1885 by J. E. K. Studd, who was invited by Moody to one of his student conferences. This aroused great interest and helped towards developing a national missionary movement among students there. Amongst other important results of the visit was the conversion of J. R. Mott, who came to personal faith in Christ in an interview with Studd the day after he had spoken at a meeting. The moving spirit was Robert Wilder, a quiet, scholarly Princeton student, who in 1886 became the main influence in starting the 'Student Volunteer Movement' in the States. He was very able and a good speaker, but he won his men more by personal friendship and personal conversation, and as soon as anyone was committed to the missionary cause he was persuaded to rope in others also. Wilder was a great man of prayer and was enormously helped by his sister, Grace, who was also a student and a really remarkable prayer warrior. They had prayed and worked for a missionary movement since 1883, but it had remained local.

Others had been concerned too and now they prayed for 1,000 missionaries. In the first year, 1886-7, the SVM enrolled 2,106 students (not all went overseas, of course); one of the earliest to enrol was John R. Mott. The SVM members signed a declaration, 'It is my purpose, if God permit, to become a foreign missionary.'[23] This was intensely personal. Almost from the start they adopted also a Watchword: 'The evangelization of the world in this generation.' This, by contrast, gave a world-wide vision, which was something new. They did not mean the conversion of the world, but they did mean the evangelization of the world *in this generation*. It gave tremendous urgency to the task and for twenty years the Watchword was to prove a major source of missionary challenge in student circles the world over. Wilder, and then Mott, carried it everywhere in their extensive travels.

We have to remember that the idea of University graduates going abroad as missionaries was rather new. A very high proportion of missionaries had been very simple folk with little education, and to become a missionary was regarded as a step down the social scale which was a disgrace to a middle-class family. That any large number of outstanding students should offer was revolutionary. That was partly why news of the Cambridge Seven caused such a sensation in America as well as in Britain. But as an American student put it: 'We had been asleep as to the subject of foreign missions, while this earnest group at Princeton (Wilder, *etc.*) had been studying the urgent needs of lost souls all over the world, and praying earnestly for them and for an awakening in American colleges to meet these needs.'[24] Revival of Christian life among students and missionary recruiting went hand in hand and their prayers in both directions were remarkably answered. Their preaching combined evangelism with a call to full consecration and to missionary service all rolled into one. So many students were nominal, orthodox Christians and they needed life.

Willingness to go to the mission field became almost a test of the reality and vividness of faith. American Christian student life had been dramatically awakened by this volunteer movement, rather in the same way as the Cambridge Seven had affected Britain. The difference was that in the USA they had kept it up through a good, but modest, organization and a roll of people who signed the volunteer declaration.

The Student Volunteer Missionary Union

In 1891 Wilder came to Britain on his way to missionary service in India. At the Keswick Convention he was given thirteen minutes in which to speak. He closed amid shouts of 'Go on! Go on!' and was besieged by students. He made a marked impression on the CICCU President and Secretary and other CICCU leaders (Keswick was nearly always well attended by CICCU men). He also touched student leaders from other places.[25] Donald Fraser from Glasgow had been converted from virtual agnosticism at the start of the Keswick week and was now called to the mission field through Wilder's speech. The CICCU men invited Wilder to Cambridge in 1892, when he spent a week there and spoke with great power. He launched the use of the SVM declaration, which was accepted after considerable hesitation. Other Keswick contacts had arranged for him to visit Aberdeen, Glasgow and Edinburgh and he was well received everywhere. His message was one of entire consecration, evangelistic and missionary zeal and the necessity of the work of the Holy Spirit if anyone was to become like Christ.

Fifty-four Cambridge students wrote to the CMS following Wilder's visit. A Cambridge man, Louis Byrde, agreed to become secretary of a national 'Student Volunteer Missionary Union' and to try to promote it outside Cambridge. Both Wilder and the Cambridge men had a national movement in mind from the start. It absorbed several other older student missionary groups, notably one in London. Byrde's room in Corpus Christi College became an astonishing hive of activity, with correspondence coming in from all over Britain. Two thousand letters are still preserved. Byrde was also a great man of prayer, with a contraption of string and weights to remove his bedclothes and so get him out of bed at 6 a.m. each morning for prayer and Bible study. A. T. Polhill-Turner was back on leave from China and became the first Travelling Secretary for one year. But the Union was to be essentially a 'student to student' affair.

A conference was arranged in 1893 at Keswick for a week preceding the Convention and students from quite a number of other universities were present at that. From nine o'clock to eleven each morning the time was taken up with SVMU business, but 11.30 to 1 p.m. was used to discuss the advancement of Christian Unions in the Universities of the British Isles. Missionary zeal did not neglect the home field and the leaders of the SVMU were also leaders of the growing fellowship of University CUs. The SVMU Travelling Secretary was the one person to visit extensively for the Christian cause. They immediately began to plan for an Inter-University Christian Union and in the following year adopted the name 'British Colleges Christian Union'. The SVMU Travelling Secretary reported SVMU groups in sixty colleges and with 700 members. 'We are', he reported, 'in the midst of the largest, most influential and most permanent missionary revival that Great Britain has ever seen.' The second SVMU Travelling Secretary was Donald Fraser of Glasgow. He quickly realized the need of strong CUs if there was to be a supply of men and women for the mission field. SVMU must depend on a healthy BCCU. A joint conference for the two Unions was arranged before the Keswick Convention the next year and a joint General Secretary of the SVMU and BCCU was appointed (another Cambridge man). In 1895 BCCU acquired a Travelling

Secretary of its own when Donald Fraser transferred from SVMU to BCCU.

The following year (1896) a really large-scale missionary conference was held in Liverpool. It was called the International Student Missionary Conference and was the first public event in the life of the movement. Speakers included C. T. Studd and G. L. Pilkington of Uganda ('Pilks'), who were home on leave. Over 500 men and 120 women were present and the excitement of the gathering gave a new vision. It was decided to adopt the 'Watchword' ('The evangelization of the world in this generation'). A group was set up to take the Watchword to the churches and get them to adopt it officially. Douglas Thornton and G. T. Manley (both hot from the CICCU) were sent to the Archbishop of Canterbury. The Watchword became a major factor in a growing world-wide missionary movement. Delegates were sent to the USA Conference.

In 1895 the SVMU movement world-wide led to the founding of the World Student Christian Federation, and in 1898 the BCCU began to call itself 'the Student Movement', which was the name of their new magazine. It was not until 1905 that the movement officially changed its name to the Student Christian Movement.

If this sounds a somewhat breathless series of developments, the answer must be that indeed it was. Once the movement existed at grass roots and Robert Wilder had lit the touch-paper as it were, it took only five years to grow into a national movement of both foreign and home evangelistic zeal. Wilder played a not negligible part in starting the international WSCF.

Douglas Thornton

The very speed of the process, however, had its dangers. Douglas Thornton was a firebrand whose enthusiasm recognized no obstacles. He had been an outstanding leader in Cambridge, and wherever he went he took a fishing-rod which was used, when attached to an alarm clock, to remove his bedclothes early in the morning. He was consumed with zeal for spiritual life and for the spread of the gospel. But already in 1895 attempts had been made to get speakers who were far from evangelical to address the conferences, and Thornton saw no danger in this. In fact none of these speakers could come and the movement remained firmly in evangelical hands for the time being. But the zeal for missionary recruitment and the aim of evangelizing the world 'in this generation' drove some of the leaders to brush aside theological considerations if only more men and women could be persuaded to volunteer for overseas service.

The Liverpool Conference was a turning-point. From being a largely unnoticed, grass-roots, student movement the SCM and the Volunteer Movement became known to church leaders. The leaders of SCM also turned their attention actively to cultivating the interest of church leaders, including many who were not evangelicals. In his zeal to reach everyone Thornton not only succeeded in interesting the Bishop of London but did much to draw into the movement the non-evangelical theological colleges. He worked tirelessly for a Conference of Theological Students at which the Watchword could be put before them, and in 1898 the Conference was held with 169 students and twenty-four theological college staff. Most of the Free-Church colleges were represented, but very few of the Anglican ones. It was here that the movement met a hitherto unseen problem. Thornton had proposed that, as a demonstration of their fundamental unity, the Nicene Creed should be recited together by the whole Conference and a card had been printed for this purpose. Some of the students protested vigorously because they 'were not convinced of all the truth that it embodied', and the proposal was dropped. Thornton commented afterwards that he believed that 'no one who has let the spirit of the Watchword dominate his thought and life' (one wishes that he had said 'the spirit of the gospel' or 'the spirit of the cross of Christ')could fail in the end to come to 'nearer visions of the truth in Christ'. He believed that the missionary vision that fired the movement would lead men back to unity *in the faith*. He saw that 'we cannot go and teach to men the opposites of truth'; but he was an optimist and he was proved wrong. Evangelistic zeal does not necessarily lead to biblical orthodoxy.

In 1898 the SVMU, BCCU and the new Theological Colleges Department were merged to form one movement at the insistence of Thornton and against the strong arguments of the more cautious and discerning G. T. Manley, who was then a Fellow of Christ's College. Manley feared that the merger would alter the SVMU and the CUs and lead them to lose their distinctiveness. Manley was probably the ablest-minded leader in the movement and he felt so strongly on the matter that, when outvoted, he resigned. In the long run his fears proved to be well-founded.

The Student Christian Movement

The century ended with a new situation. The SCM had become a recognized movement of importance. It was no longer student-led in the same way as it had been ten years earlier. The powerful leaders were young graduates – several of them from Cambridge. But they were moving into ecclesiastical politics where pure enthusiasm was not enough and they were easily at a loss. Their superb vision and evangelistic and missionary zeal provided inadequate safeguards. Just when the leaders thought that the movement was strong and growing so fast that it could carry all before it, the seeds of future disaster were being sown. They were over-confident and insufficiently self-critical. Numbers seemed all important if the world was to be evangelized in that generation. They could not believe that truth needed defence as well as proclamation, and in any case they were set on going abroad themselves and would have to leave the leadership to others. They believed that the missionary spirit would bring doctrinal agreement as it had, in measure, helped to bring new life.

There was also a growing link with the World Student Christian Federation. Delegates went to WSCF Conferences and WSCF leaders, particularly John R. Mott from the USA, frequently visited Britain. He was the main missioner for the CICCU in 1896, 1898, 1905 and 1908.[26] This gave a new vision, not only for evangelism world wide but for a world-wide church with its own indigenous leadership. It was a thrilling and to most people a totally new perspective. To some it became an excuse for a sort of religious eclecticism – let every man have his own view without mutual criticism. A division began to appear within the ranks of the movement's leadership – and the leadership was evangelical almost to a man. Some, like Wilder, Manley and most of the CICCU leaders, remained robustly biblical and were drawn increasingly into defending the truth as they saw it. Others, like Thornton and Mott, while not changing their own position, were so anxious to bring in everyone that they refused to contend for an evangelical position so long as everyone was zealous.

These dangers were as yet discerned by only a few. The SVMU had enormous momentum and it was very difficult to stand back and be critical when one was caught up in such a remarkable movement of zeal for the gospel and self-sacrificing service (by 1933 3,600 members of SVMU had actually gone abroad with British missionary societies and the number for the SVM in America was far larger). It was probably the greatest missionary movement among students that the world has seen. Most Christian students were having to face up to the possibility that they were called by God to go overseas and in those days overseas service was not only professional suicide, it was really dangerous to life and health in most parts of the world. A great many of the

CICCU leaders joined SVMU, though by no means all actually went overseas.

The life of CICCU members

It is possible to reconstruct to some extent the life of the CICCU men of the late '90s. At the time of writing some who were in these groups are still living, and a decade or so ago there were plenty of them to talk to. It was a day of close and lasting friendships – not of course between men and women, but within the company of your own sex. Most CICCU members spent a good deal of time in a warm circle of four to ten close friends, and a larger circle of those they met at DPM and on vacation missions, *etc.* They visited one another's homes, spent holidays together and not infrequently ended by marrying one another's sisters. These friendships held for a life-time and were enormously significant after Cambridge as people scattered into the world of the ministry, missionary work or the professions. These groups were perhaps sometimes too defensive, but they were frank and real. The College groups and the Missionary Bands were often a focus. There was considerable outreach to others who were friends from sport and work. But the Keswick influence was beginning to have the effect of making groups a little too inward-looking.

It has to be remembered, however, that most students were not sceptical. They usually believed in a general way in the truth of Christianity, and when students spoke of their faith coming alive or of a new experience of consecration it seems that it was often what we would describe as conversion or coming to a personal faith. But it did not necessarily involve a dramatic change of life. Many, like Douglas Thornton and Theodore Woods, who came from evangelical homes, did not really get going spiritually until they had a fresh experience at Cambridge or Keswick, often in their first year. Such 'newly awakened' Christians would drop their gambling and their heavy drinking, if those had been their custom. Their aim in life and their use of time and money would change; but they still had – as students usually do – plenty of natural points of contact with many non-Christians. Their cultural background was similarly religious and many of their common interests, such as sport, music, practical jokes and perhaps shooting and walking, were shared. Sport was particularly important and many CICCU men were prominent in cricket and rowing. Bicycling – sometimes tandem – was a new amusement. It was a CICCU man and his friend on a tandem who tried to break a record by riding 100 miles without a stop and were dismounted by a hump-back bridge after 99 miles. Many students walked for a couple of hours in the afternoon for exercise and pleasure. On Sundays they were often busy with Sunday Schools or Open-airs, and speaking in the Open-airs was for many a kind of crossing of the Rubicon. Once they had done that they began to speak to their friends. Personal devotions were very important. The Morning Watch was constantly emphasized and practised.[27]

Prayer was very important and informal corporate prayer in small groups was the norm. Small, purely social, tea-parties often ended in prayer together and the DPM was a focus and a school of prayer. Personal evangelism and persistent prayer for the conversion or spiritual blessing of friends were expected; taking friends to the Sunday evening evangelistic meeting or to the Keswick Conference was the accepted climax of it.

The rise of the Children's Special Service Mission and Scripture Union was an important factor. It was not only the encouragement of personal daily Bible study that helped, but the involvement with holiday seaside missions and camps. These were an enormous encouragement and many young converts were taken off immediately to beach missions with a Cambridge team and there pushed into public witness for the first time. A sense of spiritual responsibility for the boys who had been in your tent in the summer camp was a school of pastoral and evangelistic training for which many lived to be grateful, and it had in its turn an effect on evangelism in the University. Because a simple gospel message was seen to transform lives in the vacation, students came back with fresh confidence in the power of the gospel – but sometimes also with the feeling that fellow-students should be evangelized just as if they were school-boys. Over the years the CICCU has owed an enormous debt to this work (and *vice versa*), but has sometimes been over-influenced by the thrill of children's evangelism towards neglecting depth and critical thought.

Indeed it must be said that theological depth was not a notable feature of the CICCU in this period. Plenty of members got first-class degrees in all subjects, but as a rule study was directed more to missionary study than to theology or apologetics, apart of course from the straightforward study of the Bible. Louis Byrde, for instance, was described as follows: 'He was neither a thinker nor to any extent a reader; he was, however, a painstaking and regular Bible student, a man of prayer and a man of action.'[28] He became a first-class missionary.

During the Boer War, when Lord Kitchener was given an honorary degree in 1898, and again when besieged Mafeking was relieved in 1900, the University went wild; shutters were torn off the shop fronts and wooden railings lifted from gardens and from the Backs for a huge bonfire in the market place. But, being gentlemen, at least one CICCU member remembered going round the shops next day to offer to pay for the damage. Student pranks could be more destructive and dangerous than they are today and conflict between the 'town' and the 'gown' was still in evidence (it had been intense fifty years before). Cambridge was also an intensely male community. When in 1897 the Senate was voting on the question of admitting members of the women's Colleges to titular degrees (*i.e.* allowing them to put BA after their name if they passed their exams!),

Trinity Street was festooned with effigies of women and Caius had a banner, 'Get you to Girton, Beatrice, get you to Newnham, here is no place for maids.' But life was leisurely. Horse trams were instituted in 1880 to bring you from the station. Reputedly slower than walking, they continued until 1914. Horse buses traversed the town from 1896.

Some CICCU leaders later lamented that they were so involved in the CICCU that they had little time to benefit from the cultural and intellectual riches of student life. But often they made these criticisms from a position of great responsibility in the church or the professions, which suggests that their CICCU involvement had in fact taught them some very important lessons and given them a disciplined use of time which stood them in better stead than the often lazy enjoyment of culture and society that was the attitude of most of their peers. It would have been good to do both; but if there was not time for both it is not at all clear that they suffered any loss through choosing what they did.[29]

Chapter Four

1900 – 1910
The battle for the truth

By 1900 the British Student Christian Movement seemed from the outside to be set for a period of steady growth in size and influence. Many within the movement, however, were aware of a growing tension. On the one hand the heirs of the evangelical tradition, epitomized by the CICCU as the oldest and largest Christian Union, remained unchanged in their evangelistic, missionary, Bible exposition and devotional emphases. On the other hand there were those who increasingly clearly did not want the movement to be narrowly evangelical. Most of them - perhaps all – had an evangelical background. But they were increasingly friendly to the new liberalism of continental theology, and already by 1901 many of the SCM leaders were committed to a liberal-critical approach to the Bible. The SCM General Secretary, Tissington Tatlow, called it 'the modern view of the Bible' and described it later as 'The great movement of the Spirit manifested in . . . Higher Criticism'.[30]

Theological liberalism
The issues were not all black and white. A more *scholarly* approach to the exposition of the Bible was, in itself, good, and the older evangelicals were often too superficial. But along with this there came in, and was welcomed, a *rationalistic* approach. People began to argue that we should

acknowledge only those parts of the Bible that were intellectually acceptable. This was resisted by the evangelicals, more by instinct than by theological acumen, and they were therefore often driven by reaction into a slightly anti-intellectual stance. If scholarship led to such an abandonment of biblical truths, then they were against all scholarship. Often the new rationalistic approach meant accepting highly speculative, but clever, reconstructions of the Bible which appealed to the current evolutionary philosophy of religion. Anything in the Bible that did not fit in with such a scheme was deemed to be an error. The classical expression of this view appeared in such phrases as 'It is incredible that...', 'We cannot nowadays believe that...'. Wellhausen's very influential *History of Israel and Judah*, which had this fundamental approach but put it over with great skill, was first published in the *Encyclopedia Britannica* in 1881 (article 'Israel') and also as a book in 1885.[31] The rationalistic (not rational) principle meant that all revealed truth was to be accepted only if it could be justified at the bar of reason. Because of a strong orthodox background the first effect of this was not to throw everyone into wholesale doubt, but quietly to destroy all revealed authority. Christian truths were now spoken of from the pulpit as 'I think...', 'It seems to me that...', 'I believe...', 'I suppose we would all agree...'. The element of authority expressed in the words 'Thus says the Lord' became inappropriate. The Bible was used now to illustrate truths accepted on rational grounds, not to prove truth. Evangelicals felt the hurt most because they had relied on Bible preaching, and they reacted most sharply against it. That is to say, those who were not intellectually overwhelmed by the tide of thought reacted; sometimes they over-reacted into a rather negative attitude to all theology and all intellectual activity. But they were right in seeing that the question at issue was absolutely fundamental. Has God spoken?

Apologetics

Along with this went the question of the place that should be given to apologetics. All were concerned to answer the new sceptical spirit. Scientific materialism was beginning to be influential and many students were doubting the basic elements of Christian faith that had been taken for granted by the majority twenty years earlier, even by those who were not personal believers at all. These doubts also affected CU members. It has to be admitted that the more liberal elements in the SCM and in the CICCU – apart from G. T. Manley and a few others – were the most eager to deal with such problems. Evangelicals tended to answer with a fresh assertion of the truth; the more liberal leaders came down to sit where the doubters sat and often tried harder than others to understand and then to answer them. But because they no longer held strongly to the sufficiency and reliability of the biblical revelation, they tended to give away too much in order to keep the doubters within the movement. Apologetics has always been a dangerous occupation and this generation fell into the standard traps without realizing it. A profound optimism about human nature was accepted and made them unwary of the dangers for themselves or their hearers of not keeping close to revealed truth. They felt sure that everyone would come back to the truth in the end, because they were so good-hearted.

For a long time people of these two traditions worked together in the CICCU and the SCM. The polarization happened only gradually, but it was made inevitable by the SCM's commitment to rationalistic higher criticism of the Bible. By 1901 it was accepted by many SCM leaders and by 1906 this was open and more or less official; but even in 1900 some leaders saw the nature of the coming conflict.

Causes of weakness

The evangelicals of the older school tended to tackle all problems by direct biblical preaching. The Keswick devotional emphasis and concern about sanctification and a personal experience of the work of the Holy Spirit held the major place in their programme. To such people the academic theological debates about the Bible seemed unprofitable. At a crucial stage they also lost some of their more scholarly leaders from the student scene. Handley Moule, who was a model of accurate exposition and had enormous influence in Cambridge, became Bishop of Durham in 1901. He was then largely taken up with diocesan affairs for which he was not specially gifted. In any case he was no longer in Cambridge and he was not replaced by anyone of like calibre. In Oxford also F. J. Chavasse, who was in many ways a similar leader to Moule, accepted the Bishopric of Liverpool in 1900. Both had run crowded weekly Greek Testament expositions and had helped many to care for conservative and scholarly handling of the sacred text in a truly devotional and, at the same time, biblically and theologically accurate way. Moule's dictum, 'There should be no such thing as undevotional theology or untheological devotion', was an ideal that few others followed. The younger 'intellectuals' tended to expound the Bible less and to try to grapple with 'problems'. Speakers tended to be either devotional *or* theological, and if theological to be commonly influenced by rationalistic liberalism. If Moule and Chavasse had stayed on in Cambridge and in Oxford respectively for fifty-three years as Simeon had done, the history might have been very different.

Another factor was that many of the best leaders, including some of the most shrewd thinkers, went abroad as missionaries. Douglas Thornton had left for Egypt by 1898 and died of typhoid in 1908. Pilkington had died in Uganda in 1898. G. T. Manley and Robert Wilder were in India and in those days could not even be adequately consulted. When these missionary leaders came back to speak in CUs and at conferences they were inspiring and challenging, but no longer in close touch with what was going on. Those who were left to run the SCM and the World Student Christian Federation were not all so clear-headed theologically, although they retained their evangelistic zeal and the emphasis on prayer. A historian has recently affirmed that one of the main reasons for the decline of 'the evangelical party' in the Church of England in the latter part of the nineteenth century was that their best minds were buried (either literally or metaphorically) in the malarial swamps of Africa, leaving theological teaching and leadership to anyone else who liked to take it on.[32] And of course missionary casualties were high. The cause (let alone the cure) of malaria was only discovered in 1895. The average life of the Bishops of Sierra Leone was at one stage not much more than two years. This missionary blood-letting was their glory and the foundation of evangelical churches all round the world. Indeed without the missionary zeal there would have been relatively little evangelical blood in the veins. It need not, and should not, have led to weakness at home. But evangelical leadership was nearly overwhelmed in the events of the next fifteen years and one is bound to say that one reason was the lack of a sufficient group of the best men giving their attention to theological training and biblical theologizing.

It is possible for us, with the wisdom of hindsight, to see some of the things that went wrong. But we must confess that we should easily have made the same mistakes and that we must learn from the past. Liberalism seemed to be a way of making Christianity more acceptable and relevant to the new scientific generation. Most of those who went liberal did so believing that they had to move from the old position because of modern discoveries. They also believed that the shift would enable them to win over those who were abandoning faith because of the sceptical and rationalistic spirit of the age. As has often happened before, they absorbed the ideas that they set out to combat. The leaders of this movement themselves became rationalistic in order, so they thought, to combat rationalism.

The SCM was progressively taken over by liberal theology so that evangelicals found it impossible to maintain their position within it. In fact, apart from the CICCU and isolated individuals, the whole student movement including the High-Church section was overwhelmingly swept into the liberal net. It was soon possible for people to argue that anyone holding to the traditional orthodoxy was simply not an educated man.

The inclusive principle

The trouble for the student world started with inclusiveness. The Watchword of the SVMU, which was not after all a biblical idea in itself, pushed people to take risks for the sake of numbers. If the gospel was seriously to be preached throughout the world in that generation, then the *number* of missionaries seemed to be all-important. Membership of SVMU was carefully watched and advertised. Everyone began to care too much about the size and influence of the movement. To be caught up with 'the spirit of the Watchword', to use Thornton's phrase, became for some a sort of special 'experience' that reduced critical thought and brushed aside all opposition. It did not induce in most people a renewed concern for the content of the gospel.

Secondly, the involvement with the theological colleges, where continental liberalism had become influential, brought what Tatlow called 'the modern view of the Bible' on to the SCM platform. Next a great effort was made to get the High-Church colleges and the 'High-Church Party' and 'Broad-Church Party' leaders to take an interest in the Watchword and later in the movement.[33] The attempt to get the churches to adopt the Watchword failed, partly because most of the Church of England leadership was not evangelical and suspected anything from that source. Tatlow, and Mott on his frequent visits to Britain, realized this and therefore worked hard to get the Archbishops and other official leaders interested and to broaden the theological base of SCM so as to make it more widely acceptable. In order to do so they asked non-evangelicals to speak at the conferences. By 1900 there was beginning to be controversy about speakers. In 1903 G. T. Manley and three other missionaries home on furlough asked the leaders to restore the evangelical emphasis at the conferences. In 1904 another group of senior friends, including E. S. Woods, wrote similarly. Canon Webb-Peploe, a leading evangelical minister, wrote to the secretary expressing doubts about appearing on the conference programme as an alternative speaker to men of other outlook. The office of the SCM was bombarded from all sides asking them to have more evangelicals, more High-Churchmen, or more liberals, according to the standpoint of the writer. It was quickly accepted, however, that the movement was theologically inclusive and that evangelicals could no longer expect to dominate it, let alone have the platform to themselves as they had done ten years before.

The actual sequence of events, or rather trends, was not a simple one. The different factors interlocked. The attempt to be inclusive of the High-Church party broke the evangelical dominance and started a *self-conscious* inclusivist policy. The High-Church leaders who were willing to come in, however, were not usually liberal at the beginning. Theological liberalism slipped in almost unnoticed at first from the theological colleges. It was only when the inclusivist principle was accepted and acknowledged that the presence of liberal speakers was defended on the same grounds as the presence of High-Churchmen. In 1910 the SCM General Secretary, Tissington Tatlow, wrote to a protesting London medical student: 'It is part of the Student Movement position that the movement, as such, does not determine what is orthodox and what is unorthodox. We must live off the life of the Christian bodies which are composing the movement . . . I do not know of any teacher of the Bible who commands a wider following among theological students at present than Dr Peake (of *Peake's Commentary*, a Primitive Methodist who caused the protest by his talk at a summer conference) . . . his views on the Bible are those that are taught in almost every theological college in the British Isles.'[34]

At first Eugene Stock, the very influential Editorial Secretary of the CMS, was anxious about what was happening, but Tatlow managed to persuade him that all was well. The CMS was concerned because so many of their missionaries came from the CICCU, but Stock and others in CMS did not see that the rift had far wider implications.[35]

Contrasting stances

The point must be made that it was only very gradually that the different views came to be crystallized out into contrasting 'stances' like this. The letter quoted above, however, shows how things were moving in the SCM and where they ended up by 1910. By that date there was a deliberate refusal to hold to any particular theological position and an equally deliberate agreement to give prominence to whatever was prominent in the churches. By the same date many of the orthodox evangelicals realized that they must stand clearly and unequivocally for biblical orthodoxy and that this meant going in a different direction from the national SCM and the world-wide WSCF.

There was one other change that turned out to be of major importance. In 1897 the SCM conference had been moved from Keswick, partly in order that speakers of other theological outlooks would be more likely to come.[36] It was rightly felt that Keswick, with its strongly evangelical tradition, would discourage some from speaking. This greatly reduced the Cambridge attendance at SCM conferences. Most Cambridge men still went to the Keswick Convention and perhaps also to the joint CICCU/OICCU conference. Not so many came to the SCM summer conferences at Curbar, Matlock, Baslow, *etc.* (and finally, from 1912, at The Hayes, Swanwick, which was acquired primarily for the SCM).

CICCU and SCM

The result of all this was that the CICCU avoided being drawn into the growing eclecticism of the SCM. Some of its leaders were involved and were influenced that way, but they were few. It so happened that there were not so many old CICCU men in the SCM leadership at this time, although there were several leading OICCU members. The very influential secretary of the SCM, Tissington Tatlow, was a Dublin man who did not understand Cambridge and became increasingly an ecclesiastical politician. He was not the first nor the last evangelical to have lost his critical faculties under flattery and in the company of those who were counted great in the churches. In his official history of the SCM he repeatedly confesses that the initiatives were going more and more to senior friends of the movement rather than to the students and he also reveals how important it was for him to talk with prominent church leaders. Some of these friends, such as Bishop Charles Gore, had never been in a CU and some who had were no longer of the same spirit or doctrine because they had been absorbing liberal theology.

By 1905 there was not only conflict in the SCM, there was in particular tension between the student-led CICCU, which was still of course the Cambridge branch of the SCM, and the SCM national leadership. At the grass-roots level all over the country many students came up from evangelical churches and homes, but they had little power outside Cambridge. A doctor at King's College Hospital, London, wrote of the wishes of a London Medical Students Committee: 'The Committee want more of the "old stuff", they want more of the younger speakers – people with the cutting edge still left on, even if it is a bit jaggy. A good many keen people of the evangelical way have said to me lately that they had taken younger friends to Baslow (the SCM summer conference) to get conversion hot; but the friends hadn't had it, so "next year I'm going to Keswick". I've heard that a good many times and it makes me rather sad ... I think the committee's aspirations are summed up in the idea of more Robert Wilder theology' (Robert Wilder came on to the British SCM staff from 1906 until 1915). The same letter also says: 'I am not so sure that we ought to address our Mother the Movement quite so haughtily.'[37] Mother SCM was evidently beginning to be above criticism.[38]

Between 1905 and 1910 the conflict between the CICCU and the national SCM became more explicit. They were not only pulling in different directions; they were beginning to doubt whether they could continue to work together. The CICCU was strong. In 1903 there had been an outstanding Mission with Prebendary Webb-Peploe leading. Comparisons were made with the Moody Mission of 1882 and, as in that Mission, not only were many non-Christians converted, but many Christians were greatly helped. It was straight, hot, biblical preaching. The first sermon was on 'the wages of sin is death; but the gift of God is eternal life through Jesus Christ our Lord'. Webb-Peploe was over sixty and represented the older evangelicals, but had remarkable ability to reach students. He held a short after-meeting each night and then invited men to stand to confess their new-found faith. He encouraged them to be bold and to put a memorial card, indicating their profession, on display in their rooms. The DPM took on a new lease of life and a year later the Principal of Ridley Hall spoke of 'a great wave of blessing which has come upon us'. Many Christians learnt to take a definite stand.

Evangelism in and out of term-time

CICCU members were still much involved in the SVMU, even if they played little part in the other sections of the SCM. In 1904, for instance, twenty-six Cambridge men went on one of the SVMU missionary campaigns in Huddersfield, where the aim was to win volunteers for the mission field from the churches. They also had fresh interests of their own. Apart from the Sunday School and open-air preaching in the suburbs and villages all round Cambridge and the involvement with the CSSM (now Scripture Union) in the summer, they started the Cambridge University Mission in Bermondsey. There were a good many 'settlements' and missions, run often by High-Church groups, but this mission provided both a boys' club and a dispensary and also gave priority to direct evangelistic work in a way that was true of few of the others. For the next sixty years it also provided a field of vacation service that was a help to those many CICCU men who took part, and a means of reaching totally unchurched young men from a slum area. An impressive number of future ministers, teachers and missionaries (including at least one missionary bishop) were very poor boys from Bermondsey reached through the CUM.

In 1905 there was a remarkable evangelistic week-end with the American evangelist Charles Alexander and then, in the same year, another Mission led by Dr John R. Mott. Mott was by then the chief moving spirit of the WSCF and a powerful force in the British SCM. Dr Mott was an evangelical and a good student evangelist. His own theological position never changed explicitly but as he got older he became less decisive and definite, while Robert Wilder, who had first brought Mott into the work, remained a staunch evangelical with a clear and incisive biblical ministry. By this stage Mott could not see the importance of keeping the movement solidly evangelical. A deputation from the CICCU called on him and begged him to use his influence in the WSCF to preserve its evangelical heritage. Mott could not see the point. Indeed it seems that privately he was definitely against this policy. He was already set on an inclusivist course whose success he seemed to see all around the world in the growing number of students in the WSCF. He continued to push the British SCM in that direction and his own overwhelming personal influence was hard to resist. In Cambridge, however, he was accepted as an evangelist and at this stage at least did not alter the pattern of CICCU activity.

'The majority of the devoutly Christian young men in Cambridge are probably evangelical in their views' was a contemporary comment in the *Church Quarterly Review*. High-Church influence was weak in Cambridge, whereas Oxford was its focus. There was, however, a growing group of senior men who were willing to speak for the CICCU, though many of them were not really of the same theological outlook. Montagu Butler, the Master of Trinity College, had been helped in the CU as an undergraduate and loved to expound the Bible, but he would not preach on the atonement because he did not really understand it. He too had been a teacher at 'Jesus Lane', but he must have been something of an exception to the staunch orthodoxy of the majority of that group. R. H. Kennett, the Professor of Hebrew, was becoming increasingly clearly a liberal in his view of the Bible and later his view of the atonement, but he was also willing to speak for the CICCU. There were no senior men of a strongly evangelical orthodoxy to take the place of Handley Moule and the several professors of science who had helped during the Moody Mission and the Cambridge Seven period. The CICCU was accustomed to senior help and appreciated it and accepted these men as speakers without much criticism.

Deepening division
At the same time a growing group of young University

teachers became critical of the CICCU's narrowness and tried to persuade the leaders to broaden out. After a while, they began to discuss the possibility of creating a new SCM branch in Cambridge which would enable them to get more speakers of other points of view on to the platform. In Cambridge itself, the senior pressure was all for an inclusivist policy. Webb-Peploe and most of the regular CICCU speakers and friends in other parts of the country repeatedly urged them to stand firm. Ridley Hall was going somewhat liberal and Holy Trinity and the other churches were not a strong influence either way. In 1905 a number of seniors took a separate initiative and invited Father Ball of the Community of the Resurrection (strongly High-Church) to lead an independent Mission in Great St Mary's Church. The CICCU was invited to support. It was said that Ball believed in conversion and would preach for it, and the CICCU was at first inclined to agree. They had never faced this sort of co-operation problem before and had little experience to guide them. The matter was settled, however, when G. T. Manley (who was home again from the mission field) gave the week-end Bible reading on justification by faith. Issues at stake were spelt out and the CICCU decided not to support the Mission. They were publicly criticized for this by the Bishop of London and others, but when the Mission actually took place, most of the evangelicals realized that the decision had been right. The missioner did not mean the same thing as they did by conversion or the means of entering and growing in the Christian life.

In 1905 also, at the last of the series of twenty-eight joint CICCU/OICCU conferences, the OICCU shocked their Cambridge counterparts by suggesting that the CUs be broadened to enable Unitarians to accept membership. This was the inclusivist principle gone mad and was contrary to the SCM policy of the day, but it made the CICCU realize what was the direction of the policies outside Cambridge.

Reform?

In 1907, '08 and '09, the CICCU Presidents were actively involved in the SCM central activities and were all asked to help to bring the CICCU into line. These three 'reforming Presidents' in turn became enthusiastic for that task. But they could not carry the CU leadership or membership with them. It remained staunchly evangelical and preferred to maintain its own style and programme.

It is significant that, with all these pressures, the CICCU refused to lose its evangelical identity. If one asks how they managed to stand firm when the OICCU and other CUs did not (with the partial exception of the London medical schools), the answer must be that the biggest factor was that they were men steeped in the Bible. They read and studied the Bible avidly. They had also been careful to invite as speakers only those who would faithfully expound Scripture, and they made sure that their programme provided a healthy biblical diet. The SCM always suspected that it was the pressure of the CICCU's senior friends that held them, but, although such friends did urge loyalty to 'the old paths', they had less opportunity of influence than the concerted efforts of senior men in Cambridge, a succession of three 'reforming' Presidents in a row and the arguments of nearly all the national SCM leaders. By the grace of God the CICCU members stood firm for a witness to biblical orthodoxy because they were constantly exposed to the Bible at both a personal and corporate level. It has repeatedly happened in the history of evangelical movements that those outside them have attributed their stubbornness and consistency to some outside influence. That is almost the only explanation available to those who do not believe that if you keep on reading the Bible in a humble and teachable spirit, you keep on coming independently to the same conclusions. It is sincerely believed by those outside that there must have been some such overwhelming power to prevent the CICCU following a broader and looser policy. But the

College reps and the vast majority of the members were solidly evangelical. They studied the Bible daily for themselves and in informal groups and the week-end Bible readings and sermons gave them a consistent biblical theology. The reforming Presidents could not swing the general body of the student members.

Partly because the CICCU was so solidly biblical, people who held strongly to other outlooks did not join it in large numbers, and in 1906 some of those dissatisfied with the CICCU formed a new religious society, the Cambridge University Church Society. It was broadly Church of England and its published aim was 'to promote and consolidate the work of the Church of England in Cambridge'. It grew rapidly to a membership of 600 – far larger than the CICCU. There was also a Non-Conformist Union created about this time. The CICCU was therefore no longer the sole student religious society and not even the largest, though its active membership was probably comparable to that of the others. The creation of these societies also had the effect that some enthusiastic Christians of other traditions did not attempt to influence the CICCU from within. There was an overlap of membership with the other societies, but in other Universities, where the CU was the only major religious body, the pressure to broaden out often became stronger because there was nothing else for people to join. Unless a CU stood very firm, as the CICCU did, a process of gradual dilution was hard to avoid. If they stood firm other societies were likely to arise in the highly religious world of a place like Cambridge. But nowhere else were they firm enough to avoid progressive compromise of what had been a stoutly biblical tradition.

Three alternatives

Broadly speaking, three alternatives presented themselves. The first was that the CICCU should enter into some sort of federal union with the Church Society and the Non-

Conformist Union. The second was that the CICCU should come into line with the rest of the SCM and broaden its basis and platform. It soon became clear that, if this happened, a far from negligible section of the CICCU would probably leave and form a new CU. The third was that the CICCU should disaffiliate from the SCM and leave the SCM free to start its own new branch in Cambridge with the enthusiastic backing of quite a considerable group of seniors.

In 1908 experiments were carried out in the direction of the first solution. Dr John R. Mott came up for his fourth and last CICCU Mission.[39] This time, however, it was jointly sponsored by a council drawn from all the religious societies. The first of the reforming Presidents, R. L. Pelly, was enthusiastic about this policy. Outwardly this was an extremely successful Mission. It had superb publicity. The Bishops of London and Ely signed a message commending the Mission. The Guildhall was filled every night and Mott had an after-meeting each time and on the last night asked men to stand, signifying their response. He commented, 'After each evangelistic appeal a large number of men accepted Christ.' Mott's appeal had perhaps shifted a little from his earlier 'to accept Christ as their personal Saviour' to a new emphasis on 'to follow Jesus Christ'. But there was no repudiation of his evangelical emphases. One hundred and fifty gave in their names in token of decision. It was said that 'over three hundred men decided for Christ as a result of the campaign'. But the results were disappointing. The follow-up was very thorough and the CICCU's public reputation had probably never been higher, but very few of the converts stood firm and gradually lethargy set in. DPM attendance fell very low. Bellerby, the third reforming President, became convinced that the remedy was to broaden the platform even further, drop the Open-airs and perhaps drop the DPM in favour of more formal intercessions. The preachers at Sunday services became mixed in their theology and sometimes the CICCU joined with other societies to hear famous non-evangelical preachers such as Bishop Charles Gore.

No-one of that generation had seen the CICCU in its former strength. But G. F. B. Morris, the Vice-President, and a number of strongly evangelical friends became thoroughly disillusioned. They included some sons of the 1882 generation who had at least heard of greater days – Stanley Smith's son and J. E. K. Studd's son were among them. It seemed to them that the CICCU was now so uncertain in its witness that unless it could be restored to a consistent biblical ministry it had better be abandoned. They began to think in terms of a new body independent of the SCM, because they did not see how else to realize their vision for a really clear evangelical witness again.

Tissington Tatlow, from his own account of the matter, did not treat it very seriously. His friends in SCM agreed. Tatlow had by that time taken the bit between his teeth and was heading vigorously in the direction of an increasingly inclusivist policy. He regarded the CICCU's stubborn evangelicalism as little more than a nuisance. Once it was out of the SCM, the SCM leaders expected the CICCU to wither away. Tatlow made up his mind in favour of disaffiliation. His own words are: 'I was asked by the General Committee (of SCM) to spend some time in Cambridge and decide whether it seemed wiser to advise the breaking of affiliation, or to make a further attempt to bring the CICCU into line with the student movement. I spent a great deal of time in Cambridge . . . and in the end advised disaffiliation.'

The President, Bellerby, believed, however, that there was still hope and corresponded further with the SCM. Finally he decided that the question must be brought to a decision one way or the other. Tatlow was asked to come up again and address a general meeting of the CICCU, after which the matter would be put to a vote. Bellerby wrote: 'I had complete confidence that Tissington Tatlow would win the day for what I wanted – a bigger Christian Union reaching a bigger circle of men.' He hoped that the CICCU would follow the recent example of the OICCU, who had accepted the SCM's inclusive policy (though, in the event, only temporarily).

The parting of the ways

The meeting took place in March 1910. Tatlow spoke in favour of broadening the CICCU. A long discussion followed, but to Bellerby's surprise the motion was defeated and that meant disaffiliation. The CICCU General Committee met soon after to make a formal decision. To quote the CICCU Secretary: 'A tremendous discussion took place, with a real fight on the part of those desiring retention of affiliation to reverse the decision of the previous vote. For a long time the issue hung in the balance.' In the end it was decided by seventeen votes to five to stand by the decision of the previous general meeting. The SCM was sent a formal notice that 'The CICCU decides to break affiliation with the SCM' in order that both sides should be free to work unhindered in Cambridge. Morris became the President, to be followed soon after by Howard Mowll who had also been through the debate. They knew what they stood for.[40]

Thus the CICCU parted company with the SCM which it had done so much to create. To the astonishment of many, over 200 men stood by the CICCU, even though they thereby broke with a world-wide World Student Christian Federation of over 150,000 members. They were regarded either as a pathetic remnant of a once great tradition now on the way to extinction or, alternatively, as a valiant band of modern reformers, representing a challenge to others to stand for the truth against all the concerted influence and wisdom of the clever and powerful leaders of the church. In fact there were, on a very small scale, analogies with the stand of Luther. They were going back to the original tradition which had created the CICCU. They were going back to that because they believed it to be biblical. There are echoes in this story of Luther's assertion, 'My conscience is tied to the Word of God. Here I stand, I can do no other. So help me God.' It may seem impertinent to make the comparison. No-one is suggesting that their stand was as important as that of Luther, but they were, on a very small scale, in the same tradition. They did not face personal danger for their stand. They only faced looking stupid and, what is often hard to a student, appearing to be terribly old-fashioned, stuck-in-the-mud and out of touch with reality. They also faced the need to disagree sharply with personal friends and others with whom they had previously worked happily in Christian fellowship and witness. They challenge us in every generation to be willing to take a strong stand for an apparently unpopular and even hopeless cause for the sake of loyalty to God's revealed truth, to risk friendship, reputation and the glory of being part of a successful cause because of our faith in God and His gospel. They were trying to be loyal to what they found written in the Bible, even though they were in a tiny minority of educated Christians. At the time there was no glory, only an anxious testing of different possible paths; no certainty of success or influence on anyone else, only an awareness of being very much criticized by many whom they respected; no sense of creating history, only a conviction that they were following the path of duty.

Chapter Five

1910 – 1920
'Not as pleasing men . . .'

Once disaffiliated from the SCM, the CICCU seemed to be hopelessly isolated. Neither did it see any spectacular growth; in fact its membership declined slightly. Its ministry, however, was now consistent. People were being converted and built up in a biblical faith. Missionary zeal increased. But there was no revival. The SCM founded its own branch in Cambridge after an interval; but meanwhile it worked with a joint Committee of the other existing religious societies (the Church Society, the Non-Conformist Union and the very High-Church Societas Trinitatis Confraternitas). Many links of friendship were maintained with the SCM. Evangelical speakers appeared with others at the SCM Conference. Robert Wilder, whose theology never wavered, was a member of the SCM staff now, but was a welcome visitor to the CICCU on frequent occasions. R. L. Pelly, the first of the 'reforming Presidents', was also on the SCM staff and was clearly pulling hard in the opposite direction.[41] Many old friends regretted the breach and could not believe that it was necessary. Some criticized vigorously, but the liberal leaders in Cambridge had the wisdom not to try to put pressure on the CICCU. They had too much respect for the duty of every man to follow his own conviction – a situation that changed considerably after the First World War.

Most observers found it acutely disappointing that a movement with the missionary tradition of the CICCU seemed to be turning its back on the opportunity of influencing the really big, world-wide and powerful movement that the SCM had now become. The CICCU seemed a mere backwater. The theological colleges, and therefore the younger leadership of the churches, were rushing into liberalism without any idea of how destructive this was going to prove to be. They repeatedly affirmed that old-fashioned evangelicalism had no future. Most of the once-conservative High-Church leaders, like Bishop Gore, were now also at least mildly liberal. They had accepted the liberal (rationalist) principle that human reason was as valid a source of our knowledge of God as the Bible and 'Tradition'. This meant in effect, of course, that they accepted only as much of the Bible and of Tradition as 'the modern mind' could find acceptable; and that proved to be less and less as time went on. The whole Protestant world seemed to have been swept away. That some old-fashioned Church of England parishes, the Brethren, isolated Free Churches and a few students in Cambridge should hold fast was of little consequence. Even the Free Church of Scotland followed the trend. That God continued to bless the old gospel and to make strong Christians through a conservative biblical ministry was not at first so obvious as to excite comment in liberal circles. At this distance it is also hard for us to realize how much of the fruits of a biblical upbringing most of the liberal leaders retained. They still read the Bible for themselves. Prayer was very important. Their devotional life was strong and missionary work and home evangelism attracted much self-sacrifice and zeal. The situation was far from black and white, and it polarized only gradually. It took unusual discernment to see the difference between preaching that was really dependent upon an authoritative Word of God and preaching that used the Bible more to illustrate themes which had been arrived at and accepted on rational authority.

Many evangelical students could say little more than that the new theology omitted major emphases that they thought biblical, and even central, and that its denigration of the unique authority of the Bible was disastrous. They were not necessarily good apologists, but they were evangelists and knew what they and the new Christians needed and had found in the hurly-burly of student life. They preached and tried to obey an authoritative Word of God. To do less was to betray their commission. They could see that the truth of the gospel was at stake.

By capturing the theological colleges, and then the SCM, theological liberalism achieved a period of domination of the church. If it had also captured the CICCU the future of the relatively thin line of robust evangelical ministry would have been further gravely weakened. The pressures to conform are so strong in the student world that it is likely that it would have taken a long time before a strong strain of biblical evangelicalism would again have emerged.[42] There would no doubt always have been individuals and small groups who refused to bow to the theological fashion. In fact, the CICCU not only itself provided a steady flow of strong evangelical ministers and missionaries, but before long it had provided a major contribution towards the vision and the courage needed to help create similar distinctively evangelical student groups all over Britain and then all round the world. Of the twenty-five members of the 1911 General Committee, for instance, twelve became missionaries, seven others were ordained at home. Of these nineteen, five became Bishops. That generation in the CICCU included some of the outstanding evangelical Church of England leaders of the '30s and '40s at home and abroad.

Basis of Membership
Gradually the gap between the CICCU and the national SCM widened. There was considerable unhappiness with

the way things were going in some of the SCM branches. They were usually still called Christian Unions and in 1910 had still the same Membership Basis as that of the CICCU. But the leadership was increasingly in older and definitely 'inclusivist' hands. The great idea was to produce a 'synthesis' of different traditions. Evangelical speakers became fewer at both central and local levels. Bible study outlines and similar literature produced by the SCM were increasingly boldly liberal in approach. Positive discrimination against evangelicals in certain ecumenical contexts was more frequent.[43] Finally the drift of things was shown by another alteration in the SCM Basis of Membership. In 1902 the old Basis of the BCCU and SCM, 'A belief in Jesus Christ as God the Son and only Saviour of the world' had been changed after long and excited debate to the CICCU Basis, 'I desire in joining this Union to declare my faith in Jesus Christ as my Saviour, my Lord and my God.' It had been a relief to discover that this provided an acceptable solution in a tussle over the rather blunt statement of the earlier Basis. At that stage those who wanted a more open Basis had been defeated. In 1910, however, the phrase 'Jesus Christ as ... my God' was found to be objectionable, and after prolonged debate it was changed in 1913 to one that avoided a statement of the deity of Jesus Christ. It was argued not only that doubters should be in the movement, but that they should be voting members, lest they be discouraged.[44] Since no further statement was required of officers either, such people became increasingly influential in the SCM.

It is hard to over-estimate the importance of this membership question. The clear-cut call that the CICCU Membership Basis supplied, to identify oneself as in the full sense a Christian, did much to clarify its witness over the years. It was also a challenge to generation after generation of freshers to declare that they really did want to stand for their Lord in the University and acknowledge that He was their Saviour, Lord and God. It would have been easy for the

CICCU to go along with the current optimism which thought that once people were in the fellowship they would become orthodox. Perhaps the very fact that the SCM went that way helped the CICCU to see how destructive of true witness that path would be. It was so clearly part of a mood of unwillingness to stand as a body for revealed truth.

Having changed the Membership Basis in this way it was inevitable that in time the title 'Christian Union' was felt to be inappropriate to an SCM branch. Tradition, however, was strong and some CUs were, after all, older than the SCM. It was not until 1929 that the title Christian Union was officially abandoned by the SCM (in favour of 'SCM branch'), but the older SCM groups in Oxford and elsewhere had progressively dropped 'CU' long before, so that when evangelical groups were re-formed in these Universities they were usually free to adopt the old title.[45] The very idea of being a *Christian* Union with a definite Membership Basis of the kind used by the CICCU became a distinctive mark of the new evangelistic and evangelical groups that emerged in the next decade and began to distinguish them from SCM groups. In order to *help* non-Christians they had to be excluded from membership. It did not take long for evangelicals all round the country to realize that the CICCU had been right to make a break when it did or it too would have lost some essentials of a clear-cut witness.

Renewed evangelism

The CICCU meanwhile was preoccupied with its own problems and opportunities. It did nothing to try to create similar groups in other Universities. It abandoned the SCM summer conferences and went back to Keswick. Members spent their energies in evangelism and Bible study in Cambridge, including extensive Sunday School and Open-air work, and in the vacations they were involved with the CSSM and camps. The DPM increased its attendance and the Sunday sermons reached many non-Christians. There was little activity of an organized kind in the Colleges (no College Bible readings or prayer meetings), but the week-end speaker for the evangelistic sermon gave a Bible study at 12.30 p.m. on Sunday as well. This Sunday Bible reading was usually along the lines of the Keswick message of consecration and holiness and being fully yielded to God. Informal prayer among members was the rule when they met for tea and coffee, *etc.* In January 1911 it was decided to arrange another large-scale Mission and to invite Dr R. A. Torrey, an American, who in 1903 had held missions in London in which many CICCU men had assisted. Torrey usually travelled with a singer, Charles Alexander, but it was decided not to invite Alexander to Cambridge so that they should 'rely only on the power of the Word of God, without other aids to attract an audience or to lead to the conversion of souls'. Torrey came in November 1911, but there had been intense preparation – especially prayer – for nine months beforehand. Seventy members went to Keswick to prepare themselves (the membership was prob-ably around 150). The decision to bring Torrey aroused immediate antagonism in Cambridge. He was both an 'American revivalist' and also a scholarly and informed opponent of Higher Criticism. He had studied in Germany and his earlier sympathy with liberal theology had turned to determined opposition. But the CICCU asked him because he was an evangelist. There was virtually no senior support. The CICCU even had difficulty in obtaining a meeting-place owing, it was believed, to senior opposition. There was a rumoured plot to kidnap Torrey on arrival. He arrived early for preparatory meetings and urged the members to do their work 'in dependence on God, on prayer, on the Word of God and the Holy Spirit, and by personal work'. Torrey preached with logic, earnestness and spiritual power. The addresses were very simple and searching. At the end of the first week many had professed conversion and stood to signify it. Torrey stayed on another week to instruct them and to give two further evangelistic addresses. A hundred Scofield Reference Bibles were given to men who had professed conversion and Torrey's emphasis on 'the Morning Watch' led, he believed, to there being 200 men committed to spending an hour each morning in personal prayer and Bible study.

The Mission left the CICCU numerically and spiritually stronger. There were excellent speakers and crowded weekend meetings. Many of the more liberal dons, however, were offended and now regarded reunion as impossible. In particular, pressure was brought to bear on freshers in an attempt to persuade them to abandon their traditional evangelical beliefs in favour of more 'enlightened' views. Basil Atkinson, who went up in 1914, had in his first term no less than three ordained men (including the Principal of Ridley Hall) trying to argue him out of his conservative faith.

CICCU men attended the Church Missionary Union weekly meetings as well as the activities of the SVMU in fair numbers. But even these began to raise problems. The speakers at the first became theologically mixed and the SVMU, which was part of the SCM, was very mixed in membership. In the end the CICCU men formed the Cambridge Volunteer Union for those intending missionary service, although membership overlapped with the SVMU for some time. The CVU had a membership declaration with a Bible clause in it and was much more definite than SVMU about the message to be taken to the mission field. The doctrine of Scripture and its authority lay behind the whole dispute in fact and this became increasingly explicit as time went on. But the deity of Christ and the nature of His atonement were in the forefront of the debate most of the time.

A doctrinal statement

The CICCU began to feel the need to be more explicit

about what it meant when members signed that Jesus Christ was their 'Saviour, Lord and God'. There were now more students around who could affirm this without meaning at all the same thing as the CICCU. The first step in this direction was the publication in 1913 of a booklet called *Old Paths in Perilous Times*,[46] which was always referred to in a friendly way as 'Prickly Paths'. This was a sort of apologia for the separate existence of the CICCU as a distinctive witness. It affirmed clearly that the CICCU was not going to accept any weakening on the deity of Christ, Christ's view of the Bible and the nature of the atonement or the lost state of man. All these truths were being doubted by Christian leaders and the booklet declared that the CICCU refused to go along with 'multi-lateral theology, the aggregate of many views', which had become the fashion. It was a reaffirmation of straightforward orthodox belief, with a short history of what had happened.

The 1914-18 War

Godfrey Buxton – a son of the Moody Mission convert – who went up in 1913 describes how he tried to reach the fifteen men who normally sat at his table in 'Hall'. He took them to sermons and finally persuaded them to come to Keswick – each one on a motor-bike, to the terror of the villages they passed through. That was in July 1914, and in August came the war, to the complete surprise of most people. The young men poured into the army and the appalling casualty lists inscribed on College war memorials contain many names of Torrey Mission converts.[47] Of Godfrey Buxton's fifteen friends, ten were killed. The University dwindled after 1915 to almost nothing. A very small group kept the DPM going for all but a short period, but that was all they could do after 1915.

The post-war generation

In 1918 wounded men began to return and tried to resume

their studies. By January 1919 the University was again in full swing. The 1919 undergraduates were an extraordinary crowd. Many were very conceited. They had won the war and they almost believed that they were the heroes the popular slogans described ('a land fit for heroes to live in'). They were also men who had been through some terrible experiences, and in reaction they were often careless of all restraint and all serious thought. Ex-service men could do a very short course for an 'ordinary degree' which required little work. University life became rather frivolous. A small group of CICCU men soon gathered for DPM. There were rarely more than fifteen of them at first, but they were deeply in earnest. Godfrey Buxton and Norman Grubb arrived, both with military decorations for bravery and both recovering from wounds – a long process when there were no antibiotics. Buxton became President, though he was on crutches and was quite often incapacitated. Grubb went through a spiritual experience which resulted in him giving up smoking and seeking to be, in a new sense, all out for God. The group became extremely zealous and they feared no man. They set about vigorous personal evangelism. Numbers at DPM gradually rose to fifty.

Liberal evangelicalism

The theological scene was drastically different from that of 1914. Liberalism was rampant. Ridley Hall and Holy Trinity Church were both now representative of a new movement, 'Liberal evangelicalism'. Its leaders were often old CICCU men; but having drunk deeply of liberal theology, they were quite explicitly different in their teaching from the older evangelical tradition – much more so than the SCM leaders of 1910. The liberal evangelicals preached for decisions of a less clear kind. Their message was still centred in Jesus Christ, but their call was more vaguely to follow Him and at times they were not explicit on His deity.[48] What following Him meant to people depended much on

79

their background. Of course there were gradations, but the men of the new school were so certain that they were right that the older evangelicals – now beginning to be called 'conservative evangelicals' by contrast – were to many of them a rather ridiculous anachronism. The Vicar of Holy Trinity (E. S. Woods, an old CICCU man whose position had now greatly changed from his student days) described how, after a sermon in his church on the atonement by R. H. Kennett (Professor of Hebrew), which must have been frankly destructive of the truth held dear by many, a faithful old Sunday School teacher came to him to offer his resignation. The 'dear old man' confessed that after that sermon he had not slept all night and the Vicar comments, 'I could hardly control my amusement.' That was the problem. To both the Vicar and his biographer consistent evangelicalism was simply funny in its tenacious adherence to the substitutionary death of Christ. That someone had been unable to sleep because he thought truth was in danger was comical. 'They identify Christianity with that little tiny bit of religious truth and religious experience which has come within the ken of themselves and their clique', Woods wrote.[49] If people did not actually attack evangelical truth, as Kennett did, they regarded such truth as just the personal fad of a few old-fashioned Christians. There might be something in it, but it was irrelevant for up-to-date people.

Nevertheless the CICCU men did not always make things easy. They attended Holy Trinity because there was nowhere better to go. But at least one CICCU man was heard, during a sermon packed with literary quotations and no Bible references, muttering to himself as he thumbed through his Bible, 'I can't find these quotations anywhere in my Bible.' E. S. Woods was typical of the best kind of liberal evangelical. He was a deeply devoted and spiritually-minded man. No-one doubted the reality of his experience. His warmth, humility and love were a blessing to many. But in his doctrine he had moved progressively in a liberal direction. He did not, like some others, deny the doctrines he had affirmed as a student, but he welcomed speakers who did. The content of his message became less and less explicitly biblical and therefore, from the point of view of the CICCU men, it lacked both clarity and divine authority. The Pastorate, still with two ordained men, followed the trend. Ridley Hall and most of the other traditionally evangelical churches and leaders were similar. By contrast the CICCU men were brash, over-dogmatic, and sometimes rude to their seniors in an attempt to be loyal to biblical truth. They were certainly not without their faults; but the liberal evangelicals had in their theology the seeds of their own dissolution and it was not long before their weaknesses began to emerge. The next generation of liberals did not have the same spiritual capital to draw on because they had been taught differently. The CICCU had, by the grace of God, a much more biblical position and, in the long run, the power and truth of the Bible were clearly seen.

The theological lecturers were now aggressively liberal and the College Deans and Chaplains had little sympathy with the CICCU, who found themselves once more on their own and in a position of being frankly despised, pitied or laughed at by the official religious establishment and the majority of those who mattered. If the future had been left to the churches and theological faculties, the evangelical witness would have disappeared from the University scene and, in due time, from many pulpits and congregations. Mercifully the CICCU was not prepared to be led by the official Christian leadership any more than by the SCM leadership. Nor were they willing to be swamped by the influence of even the best of the local churches that were available.

The SCM was comparatively strong, intellectual and well supported. Some members, however, felt keenly that they lacked certain things the CICCU could supply. They did not want the CICCU's theology, but they wanted its zeal and prayer life and whole-heartedness. They could not believe that a watered-down message was the cause of their own weaknesses. To the liberal evangelicals it seemed obvious that so long as one 'can call Jesus Lord and slave for His Kingdom', no more should be needed.[50] History has proved that that was wrong – fatally wrong – and a reading of the New Testament warned the CICCU of the fact.

'Of first importance'

When Norman Grubb was Secretary in 1919 (he left direct for the mission field in December of that year), he and the President met a deputation from the SCM to discuss whether they could join forces. The DPM was continued all afternoon that day until the CICCU delegates returned. Grubb describes it as follows: 'After an hour's conversation which got us nowhere, one direct and vital question was put: "Does the SCM consider the atoning blood of Jesus Christ as the central point of their message?" And the answer given was, "No, not as central, although it is given a place in our teaching." That settled the matter, for we explained to them at once that the atoning blood was so much the heart of our message that we could never join with a movement which gave it a lesser place.'[51]

That the atonement was the crucial issue is significant. The CICCU was set for the *proclamation* of the gospel. They had no doubt about what that gospel was, because they trusted the authority of the Bible. So they were equally set for the *defence* of the gospel. The fact that the authority of the Bible was also crucial came home to them most of all when the gospel was at stake. Grubb quoted 1 Corinthians 15:3, 4. 'For I delivered unto you first of all (*as of first importance*, RSV) that which I also received, how that Christ died for our sins according to the Scriptures; and that he was buried, and that he rose again the third day according to the Scriptures.' Through this gospel they themselves had found peace with God and new life in Christ. It was the message that God's Word, and therefore God Himself, told them to preach 'as of first importance'. Any theology that took the edge off it was not just an alternative view; it was a fatal weakening of the message of salvation and no-one who believed that could accept compromise for the sake of outward unity, friendships or theological respectability. The eternal salvation of men was at stake. No-one who saw it like that dared to alter the message, for fear that he became an enemy of men and of God. They did not deny that the liberal preachers sometimes saw conversions. So much traditional Christianity was in the background of the average ex-public schoolboy at Cambridge that the liberals were drawing on past capital. But many were not being truly converted because they had not heard a message with the divine authority and the personal application of the message of the 'blood of Christ'. Once more the CICCU men had to say: 'Here we stand; we can do no other.' They saw themselves as compelled to stand out in the most stark way for what they believed was the only message that is 'the power of God unto salvation'.

Chapter Six

1920 – 1930
Clarifying a policy

Once the CICCU had taken its stand the problems were not over. But the 1919 summer house-party at Keswick provided a factor without which there would perhaps have been shipwreck. There was no CICCU camp in 1919 as there was in subsequent years, but Mrs C. T. Studd, who was back from Africa to be with her children, had a house-party at Keswick and invited a good number of CICCU men with a few from other Universities. It was rather hard going at the start. Nothing much was being accomplished and a small group met one evening for a prayer meeting for the house-party. They had thought it might last about half an hour; in fact they finished at about 2 a.m.

Norman Grubb was one of the leaders. After an exhausting battle in prayer the meeting ended with a sense of triumph and an assurance of prayer answered, and they rose from their knees with joy. The whole atmosphere of the house-party changed. It was a turning-point for the CICCU also. As Grubb describes it, 'Faithfulness came in Cambridge, fire came at Keswick.' It was not that they had a definable, new 'second blessing' experience, but they had a new reliance on God's Holy Spirit and the plain gospel and they had been given a vision and an assurance of God's blessing. They were able to go ahead from that time with a new confidence. They were delivered from what might have become a rather negative, defensive outlook.

Many of them went on from Keswick to a very remarkable CSSM beach mission at Eastbourne, where God did an unusual work. 'For the first time I led a boy to Christ,' wrote Noel Palmer. There was a touch of revival as a great many young people professed conversion. The team returned to University in the autumn with a new confidence in the living power of God and His gospel.

The IVF and its Basis

Noel Palmer (always called 'Tiny' because of his enormous stature) had been recovering from wounds in a military hospital on the Backs since January 1919. He had been drawn into the CICCU circle and had great admiration for the friends he made there. He writes, 'I had never before seen such a group ... They were all *men* and I hated "cissies" and prigs. These men knew and understood men, were natural and wholesome in every way. The church often put me off or left me cold; they attracted me and set me on fire.' Nevertheless when he went up to Oxford at Easter 1919 he drifted spiritually. He was followed by the prayers of Cambridge friends. Norman Grubb got him rather unwillingly to go to Keswick and Eastbourne, and at Keswick his life was revolutionized. The Autumn term 1919, he wrote, 'was like another world. DPM and weekly Bible readings began at once, and we soon had about forty men meeting. My rooms were so often occupied day and night by little spontaneous prayer groups that one of the men who had been accustomed to dropping in gave up in despair, and reported that "you couldn't get into Tiny's rooms nowadays without finding 'a forest of bottoms' all round the place!" (We used to kneel to pray). Word went round that something had happened to Tiny Palmer at Wadham and that he'd gone off his head. We were lampooned in a local theatre (especially after starting open-airs at the Martyrs' Memorial). The Varsity rugger fifteen were going to throw us in the river, but the local communists drew their fire instead because they were running a huge strike meeting next to the Martyrs' Memorial.'

The result was the restarting of the OICCU with a vengeance. (It was actually called the Oxford University Bible Union for a while.) Strong links of friendship and mutual encouragement were built between the two Christian Unions in Oxford and Cambridge. Regular prayer bulletins were exchanged. This helped to give a wider vision and it was proposed to try to establish a nationwide fellowship of CUs – a plan that had been eagerly discussed at the Keswick house-party. Norman Grubb was again one of the pioneers, and in December 1919 a first 'Inter-Varsity Conference' was called in London. The name, incidentally, owed at least something to the fact that it was planned to start in the evening of the 'Inter-Varsity' rugger match at Twickenham. It was judged that more evangelical students would be in London that day than any other! The conference called together students from Cambridge, several from Oxford and London and one from Durham. Only about sixty were present (all men), but it was the start of what became the 'Inter-Varsity Fellowship' (now 'Universities and Colleges Christian Fellowship'). There and then plans were laid to start Christian Unions wherever like-minded students could be found. A letter had appeared in the religious press saying that no-one intelligent now believed in the atonement as taught by the apostles in substitutionary terms. The six members of the CICCU Exec. who were at the conference wrote a reply which was also published. They did not care whether they were considered intelligent or not; they did however affirm that they believed this truth with all their hearts and minds. The correspondence brought them into touch with students in one or two other centres. They appointed a committee to plan another conference; perhaps it could be an annual event. A few years later another CICCU man, H. R. Gough, was appointed as a Travelling Secretary to visit the groups and encourage them. In 1928 the Inter-Varsity Fellowship of Evangelical Unions was officially created to give substance to what was already in existence as small, often very small, CUs had been created in thirteen of the Universities. Between 1919 and 1933 ten out of the fifteen IVF Chairmen were CICCU men and the IVF was during all this time a major 'missionary' interest of the CICCU.

All Christian Unions were to be autonomous in the new IVF and to have no obligation to find money or other support for the national fellowship. The example of SCM made them cautious. But the bond of union was to be a Doctrinal Basis which was drawn up by a small sub-committee with the help of senior friends. All Christian Unions who wished to be affiliated to the IVF had to have a Doctrinal Basis 'substantially in agreement' with it and the CICCU put a clause in their constitution to the effect that they accepted the Doctrinal Basis of the IVF. CICCU men played an important part in this development and the idea and content of the Basis owed much to some of them. The CICCU now realized that a clear and explicit doctrinal statement was needed in a world in which almost all the great doctrines were being doubted or denied by leading theologians and church dignitaries.

The CICCU had now nailed its doctrinal colours to the mast. It stood clearly for 'the divine inspiration and infallibility of Holy Scripture, as originally given'. It also stood without qualification for 'redemption from the guilt, penalty and power of sin only through the sacrificial death (as our Representative and Substitute) of Jesus Christ, the Incarnate Son of God'. The doctrinal position seemed quite untenable to most educated Christians. The 'baiting' of CICCU men with problems about evolution, Jonah and the Flood became an entertaining pastime for many Cambridge friends. The CICCU's evangelistic zeal and devotion, however, were admired and coveted by some other groups who felt that they, perhaps, lacked in this respect. Could not the CICCU become an evangelistic arm of the SCM? The next twenty years, therefore, saw constant argument about policy and the hammering out of a view of witness which in the end made official co-operation with non-evangelical bodies clearly inconsistent.

Co-operation policy

In late 1919 the CICCU were considering another Mission when the Student Christian Movement in Cambridge announced that they were planning one for the following year. They invited the CICCU to take part. At first the CICCU refused; then they decided to come in so long as their missioner did not join in any united statement of belief. The President stressed their fear lest the University 'be edified with a code of morals to observe rather than enriched by a new life', and defined once again the Christian Union's conviction 'that the Bible as originally given is, and not merely contains, the inspired Word of God, and is the only infallible guide to faith and practice; and that all are dead in sin and unable to please God until they have turned and received atonement for sin through the death of Jesus Christ and new life through His Spirit'. It was agreed that there would be four main missioners: a Nonconformist Dr Gray; Bishop Charles Gore, who would speak in the University Church of Great St Mary's; the Bishop of Peterborough (a former CICCU President, Theodore Woods), who was invited by the liberal evangelicals and who would preach in Holy Trinity where his brother Edward Woods was Vicar; and a missioner in the Guildhall where the CICCU could have their own speaker. Time was short. The CICCU tried to get Norman Grubb's uncle, George Grubb (through whose CICCU Mission Theodore Woods had in fact been converted as a fresher), but it was too late for him to get free and suitable missioners were very few. They eventually secured Barclay F. Buxton, the President's father, who was just home from the mission field. Theodore Woods in his open letter to the University stated his aim as follows: 'I am coming among you as a Cambridge man to talk quite plainly about the things that matter most. What the world needs in these days, what each of us needs, is to understand God and His character; to realize that in His Kingdom lies the sole hope of the world, and to discover how best we can each bring our contribution to the supreme adventure of setting it up among men.'[52] Since this gave no clear indication of preaching Christ and Him crucified, and since it put the emphasis on what we could contribute rather than on the grace of God, the CICCU were not enthusiastic. They backed Buxton without qualification.

The Mission was generally considered in Cambridge to have been a great success with excellent attendance (average daily total about 2,000) and many personal talks, *except* for the CICCU part of it. Buxton was inevitably somewhat out of touch, as he had been abroad. He was not primarily an evangelist, though he was a faithful preacher of the gospel. Also, when men had begun to be convicted in the Guildhall, they frequently went off to other missioners only to get the impression that sin and forgiveness were not the major problems. The CICCU discovered the great disadvantages of a joint mission. Nevertheless the CICCU members brought their friends to a reasonably full Guildhall and a number did profess conversion, of whom some went on to lifelong service on the mission field. The Vicar of Holy Trinity wrote: 'All groups an unbounded success except the CICCU.' The CICCU knew that numbers were not so important, so long as people were born again, and they rejoiced in the real results that they saw.

The difference between the message of the CICCU and the others began to appear as a matter of whether the grace of God was central. Those who would not preach the death of Christ for our sins and in our place could not clearly preach a totally free grace of God, because they had no basis for totally free forgiveness. Without realizing it, a human contribution to salvation began to creep in. Men were asked to decide for Christ, or to follow Christ, rather than to trust in Christ as their Saviour and Lord – one who brought a totally undeserved salvation. In this the CICCU found themselves standing as clearly over against the normal High-Church teaching of the time as against the liberal teaching. That had always been the case. The liberals called the biblical doctrine of the atonement 'the theology of the slaughterhouse'. What they preached instead (largely the example and moral teaching of Christ) was undeniably popular and acceptable to their generation, but it was fatally weak as a gospel. The High-Church preaching was never so popular and it made greater demands on people, but it seemed to the CICCU often to sacrifice the truth of the finished and complete work of Christ for an offer of salvation on conditions – conditions of attendance on the ceremonies and ordinances of the church and an upright life. Works entered into it in the wrong place and again the result was that the gospel was not the gospel of free and full salvation through the death of Christ – a salvation whose reality was to be proved by good works as a response of love for Christ's complete and sufficient work done for us. Certainly many 'churchy' students were trusting in their religiosity for salvation and needed to be shown that this was not the New Testament gospel and that it offered no personal relationship to God. The High-Church preachers on the whole failed to make this clear, even though they might agree if pressed.

As a result of this Mission the CICCU lost face and lost some popular support. There was, however, one important gain. Up to this point the evangelical members of the women's Colleges in Cambridge had had no organized programme of their own. They were not officially members of the University. They were not welcome at DPM or other CICCU activities except the Sunday night sermon, where they sat on their own in the gallery. During this mission three or four women were converted through the help of Miss Dorothea Reader-Harris, who came up to sing and to work in the women's colleges for the CICCU (she later became Mrs Godfrey Buxton!). These included the President and Secretary of the Atheists' Club, who had no use for the 'soft sell' of the other religious groups. Other women were greatly helped in the Mission and there was a substantial growth of evangelical witness in the women's colleges. The Cambridge Women's Inter-Collegiate Christian Union was therefore formed and continued its stalwart witness until it merged with the CICCU in 1948.

The CICCU were disappointed that they had not seen greater things, but they were not down-hearted. It must have taken special courage to soldier on in the face of such apparent success of the liberals and such relatively little success for the faithful preaching of biblical truth. But they believed God and persevered. Regular Sunday sermons did reach non-Christians. Friends of CICCU men were being converted and a steady flow of stalwart men went on into the ministry and the professions and out to the mission field. The CICCU was ridiculed by the religious and irreligious alike and they responded by regarding other religious groups, especially the Divinity Faculty, as imparting spiritual poison. The CICCU, however, seemed small and insignificant, whereas the SCM became extremely popular with undergraduates and seniors alike. While the CICCU preachers were not well known, the SCM had famous preachers every Sunday who drew very large audiences. By comparison the Sunday services of the CICCU seemed rather insignificant. Harold Earnshaw Smith ('Annie Smith'), who was on the Pastorate team, led the CICCU in open-air services in the Market Place every Sunday night in the summer term. He was a tremendous encouragement and stimulus to positive evangelism, though it must be admitted that the CICCU were often very tactless and aggressive.

Meanwhile missionary interest in the CICCU was strong. In 1922 the Cambridge University Missionary Band was formed for those 'willing' to go abroad. Fifty-two joined, of whom thirty-five actually went abroad, and this was out of a CICCU membership of about one hundred. Similar groups were formed in the following years. 'Cambridge Prayer Fellowship' groups were also created for those graduating each year. These kept members in touch by circular letters two or three times a year and were a significant spiritual help to quite a few. They served to maintain a missionary and evangelistic vision and some CPFs have been active continuously for more than fifty years. When the CICCU became much larger after the Second World War, the CPFs were less significant and usually functioned for only five or ten years.

In 1926 the widespread hardships in the country came to a head in the General Strike. Cambridge continued as if nothing was happening, until the week itself. Then the undergraduates were nearly all enthusiastically recruited as strike-breakers. The Missionary Secretary (L. F. E. Wilkinson) spent two days shifting milk-churns at Waterloo Station ('You rolled them on their edges in a rather delicate balance and we were swimming in milk by the end of the day'). He then drove a tram with a zest and fervour that even Jehu might have admired. But when it was all over they returned to the isolated world of the University with relief. It had been tremendous fun! Most students had little interest in the social questions, but there were important questions that they did understand and had to sort out in Cambridge.

The Willy Nicholson Mission

In 1926 another joint Mission was planned. This time the CICCU (now about 200 strong) chose Stuart Holden, a London vicar of great reputation and personal charm. A small group in the CICCU were fearful that he would be too eager to be nice to the other missioners and might not therefore speak clearly enough. When he signed with the other missioners a very bland letter to the University their fears were increased. Dr Basil Atkinson (by this time an under-librarian at the University Library) set himself to pray that Holden would not come. A week before the Mission Holden had to withdraw on grounds of health! There was consternation in the CICCU, because missioners were very few and they could not think of anyone suitable who was in the least likely to be free. At the CICCU camp at Keswick that summer Earnshaw Smith had introduced them to W. P. Nicholson ('Willy Nick', as the CICCU called him) and in the end they wondered if he could be God's man for the occasion. Nicholson was a rough and ready Irish evangelist, who had been a sailor before the mast, and he had a tremendous ministry among working-class people. His preaching in Northern Ireland had had far-reaching results and led, among other things, to the starting of a CU in Queen's University, Belfast, in 1921.

The CICCU had invited Nicholson to come over for three days of Mission preparation, 'To pep us up before the Mission'. A delegation met him off the train at Euston and suggested that he should take Holden's place. Nicholson said afterwards, 'I nearly fainted. I would rather have entered a den of lions.' 'I can't talk to educated University men,' was his reply; 'I'm just a simple sailor fellow . . . but let's have a word of prayer.' So they prayed there and then on the Euston station platform and Nicholson threw his hat in the air and shouted, 'Praise the Lord!' Nicholson telegraphed to Ireland and found that the week concerned was one of the very few in the whole year in which he could be free. So his name was put by the CICCU to the united Mission committee for approval. No-one present had ever heard of him, and the one member who had and who would probably have objected could not be present that day. So Nicholson became the CICCU missioner alongside Bishop

William Temple and a prominent liberal Free-Churchman, Cyril Norwood.

Willy Nicholson was a totally different man from Stuart Holden. He was extremely hard-hitting, blunt about sin and hell, with a racy and not very cultured sense of humour. He had absolutely no fear of men and knew virtually nothing about Universities. But he knew about sin and salvation and he preached with the authority of the Word of God. At the united introductory meeting, with the President of the Union Society[53] in the chair, he upset even some of the CICCU by his bluntness. Although William Temple shook him warmly by the hand as they left the platform, the Free-Church minister appeared deliberately to turn his back on him as a public gesture. Nicholson had both stated that he had been born again on a particular date and also baldly and with little comment affirmed the whole of the Apostles' Creed sentence by sentence. As they walked away across the Market Place Earnshaw Smith said to Nicholson, 'Whatever made you do that? Now you have ruined everything.' 'Brother Smith,' replied Nicholson, 'if I had done what you thought, and pleased everybody, it would have been the end of your Mission. Now you will see. God will work.'

On the Sunday, the first day, Nicholson preached to a rather small audience in Holy Trinity Church on the text 'Ye must be born again'. Crowds attended the other missioners. But at least Nicholson was not dull. 'It was extraordinary,' said one freshman; 'very vulgar and yet – very attractive at the same time.' He lashed out against the popular idea that Christianity was just following the example of Christ. He hammered away at the biblical truth that 'You must be born again'. A few professed conversion that night. But the reputation of the missioner in Holy Trinity spread. His style and manners were very unconventional. Students came just for fun and then were either offended or convicted, though some mocked. The President of the Drunks' Club was converted – later to become Secretary of a missionary society – and brought his friends along too. Each night there were some who made a profession of conversion. And Willy Nicholson didn't make it easy. The Mission ended in a cloud of controversy, but with a substantial number of new Christians.

The issues becoming clearer

The Cambridge scene was never quite the same after that. CICCU men either left in disillusionment and joined the SCM, or they realized afresh the impossibility of compromise and the need to speak clearly of God's truth, however unpopular that might be. But the other societies were also different in their attitude to the CICCU. Many were angry that such a witness had been given in such a way. They were no longer enthusiastic for future co-operation; indeed they had little desire to be associated with that kind of Christianity. To them the CICCU seemed out of place in a University. Nevertheless attendance at the Sunday night evangelistic sermons increased. In 1928 Charles Raven, a leading liberal evangelical (who became the Regius Professor of Divinity in 1932), wrote of the CICCU, 'It is incredible that anyone with the intelligence to pass Littlego (the University entrance exam) should still believe in Jonah's whale and Baalam's ass.'[54] This sort of attitude was common.

For its part the CICCU was getting used to this kind of attack. Liberalism was becoming more and more aridly negative. Theological study did not even pretend to be much of a preparation for the ministry. It was more of an academic philosophical exercise for the solving of intellectual problems. To study theology was to enter a spiritual wilderness, personally enlivened only by a few lecturers like Raven, who was warm and enthusiastic and had great power of oratory, but very little biblical content to his lectures. Most of the CICCU men who took theology seriously became liberal and were lost to the cause. Those who survived, with a few notable exceptions, were people who laughed their way through the course and nurtured their spirits in the CICCU and in vacation evangelism among young people. There was little else that they could do. There were virtually no evangelical theological scholars who could help and no literature except what could be dismissed as long out of date.

Nevertheless in the growing fellowship of the IVF they began to find friends in other Universities. Even if there were none in Cambridge, there were University professors (notably in science and medicine) elsewhere who would come and speak. There were older men in the parishes and in the Keswick circle, too, who were willing to do all they could to help, though their number was not large. In their turn the CICCU contributed substantially to the IVF. The first four IVF Travelling Secretaries, in 1923–29, were all CICCU men.[55] Hugh Gough, for instance, who had been President of the CICCU for nearly two years (1925–27), travelled widely in the following year to help the new evangelical groups that were emerging in Universities all round the country. The incipient Manchester CU, consisting of four students, wrote of his visit in 1927: 'We felt that God had sent Mr Gough to us as an encouragement from the Evangelical Unions already formed, and we thanked God and took courage.' The following week the Manchester University Evangelical Union was launched. News of the CICCU's witness also helped in other places. They corresponded with students as far as Aberdeen and a CICCU member finishing his studies in Edinburgh contributed to the start of the EU there in 1922.[56]

At Oxford in 1928 the OICCU got going again. It had lapsed in 1925 into being the 'Devotional Union' within the SCM and that had never been a success. Now sixteen members broke away from SCM and re-started the OICCU. There was intense interest and prayer support in Cambridge following the IVF Conference where they had met.

For their first public outreach three CICCU men, including the President, Kenneth Hooker, were asked over to speak at a meeting in the Town Hall on 'What Christ means to me'. The Town Hall was packed and the OICCU was re-launched with a new confidence in God – the collection at the door exactly meeting the formidable expenses to the nearest penny! Having learnt its lesson by painful experience the OICCU quickly became an enthusiastic and robustly evangelical group again and joined with the CICCU and the LIFCU (London) in helping to found CUs all over the British Isles. If the CICCU helped to establish the IVF, the IVF helped the CICCU to remain faithful and to be more confident of the gospel. In Cambridge, where they were a despised minority, it was a help to know of friends in other Universities who stood for the same witness and policy.[57]

Oxford, Cambridge and London were the three largest British Universities. A CICCU man, Chris Maddox, became the IVF (honorary spare-time) Missionary Secretary and travelled the Unions in a minute and ancient car to stir up missionary enthusiasm. Others helped in other ways. In 1928 Norman Grubb came back from Canada and challenged the infant IVF to do something to start similar work there. An income of £20 per annum hardly seemed adequate! But the same autumn Dr Howard Guinness (Bart's Hospital, London) was sent across the Atlantic by the sacrifice of fellow-students (who sold belongings to finance the trip) and the help of Professor Rendle Short (Professor of Surgery at Bristol). Professor Rendle Short belonged to the 'Open Brethren' and was an indefatigable visitor to tiny groups of students to help CUs to get going. He was a constant visitor and speaker at Cambridge and did much to inspire the vision of a nation-wide network of Christian Unions and to give a sense of responsibility for helping other Universities and other countries. This was needed because Cambridge easily forgot everyone else, except perhaps the OICCU.

In 1929, when Howard Guinness went on to Australia, Kenneth Hooker, who had been CICCU President in 1927-8, went to Canada for a year as their first staff worker. In 1930 he was followed by 'Tiny' Palmer of Oxford for three years until a Canadian worker was found. Thus the Canadian IVF was established and later pioneered the work in USA. The foundations of the International Fellowship of Evangelical Students were being laid and CICCU members had an honourable part in helping in several countries.

Super-spirituality

During the same period the CICCU had to resist the impact of the movement led by Frank Buchman. At first it was called 'The first Century Christian Fellowship', later it was called the Oxford Group and today Moral Rearmament (MRA). It tested the CICCU's discernment to the limit. Buchman was an American of great personal charm. He arrived in 1920 and made Cambridge his base for a year. He constantly stated his faith in the whole Bible, the death of Christ and the second coming. He spoke of blessing that he had received at Keswick. But although he seemed to be biblical he rarely spoke from the Bible. He disapproved of holding a Bible or speaking from it directly, as he said it might put off worldly people. His talks were very thrilling and he had round him men and women keen to win souls by using his methods. He gave impressive reports of revival in American Universities. He was impatient of formality or unreality in religion. He stressed the need for a personal moment-by-moment experience and fellowship with the Lord, and his followers were active personal evangelists.

Buchman was at first received warmly by the CICCU. His challenge to an absolute morality was needed and was helpful. Many CICCU men owed something to his emphases. He took the CICCU week-end and one of their house-parties. As time went on, however, disturbing features emerged. He spoke of the Quiet Time, but it was less and less a time of Bible study and prayer and increasingly a time of 'listening to God'. This members did with their mind blank and with paper and pencil in hand, writing down the thoughts that came to them. In this way men received entirely irrational guidance about the most trivial as well as the most important issues, and such guidance was of course regarded as authoritative. Guidance at other times was instant and unpredictable. The leader of a student team would decide only at the last minute who should speak at the Open-air. Either this was very spiritual indeed, or it was a pious cloak for indecisiveness and a refusal to be guided by the discipline of biblical wisdom. 'Sharing', especially sharing of sins, was also a prominent feature. The whole movement sounded more 'spiritual' than anything based on the Bible. Quite often guidance was received for other people, dictating to them what they should do. Confession of sins in public became a feature and the fellowship of sinners seemed to be warmer than the fellowship of saints. But the problem came to a head when secondary issues began to take the place of the gospel. The Four Absolutes (absolute honesty, absolute purity, absolute unselfishness and absolute love) became the point of challenge to the non-Christian. The result was that, when men and women were 'changed', it often proved to be purely an attempt at personal moral revolution. Spectacular converts who spoke in public proved soon to be spectacular backsliders. Only a few seemed to be truly born again and 'the Groups' produced a fierce antagonism among non-Christians, so that Christians had to be willing to take sides. The Groups left something of a scorched earth behind them and many Christians felt they had to dissociate themselves entirely from their aggressive but biblically weak approach.

Many people in the CICCU were involved at least for a time. They tended to lose their concern for doctrine and to end up less definite about the gospel – unless they reacted out of it, as a considerable proportion did. But the unqualified challenge was a help to some – so long as they did not lose their biblical base. Gradually the CICCU and the Groups drifted apart as distinct entities and the latter shifted their emphasis to Oxford, where they were rather more successful. This gave rise to the title 'Oxford Group'. The influence continued in Cambridge for a while, however. Ivor Beauchamp (son of one of the Cambridge Seven) wrote in 1922: 'Frank Buchman held one of his week-end house-parties in John's; it was a time of real power and blessing and a great stimulus to those of us who went.' He then named two recent CICCU ex-Presidents as having been present.[58]

In 1924 Douglas Johnson, a student at King's College and later King's College Hospital, London, became secretary of the Inter-Varsity Conference. His predecessor, an Oxford man, had become favourable to Buchman. 'DJ', as he was always called, saw the danger and helped others to do so. DJ's ministry was never in the foreground; but his lively vision, clarity of principle and determination that the men on the spot should carry the responsibility, were an enormous help to many in the CICCU over a long period. A number of former CICCU leaders who were now finishing their medical studies in London were still influential in Cambridge at this time. There was a good deal of coming and going between Cambridge and London, especially the London medical schools, and DJ was in the centre of the London CU scene and the growing IVF. Many of the leaders of the new CUs had too little discernment to see the danger. DJ was one of those who did.

Harold Earnshaw Smith, who was in Cambridge for most of this period in the Pastorate and in other capacities, was another steadying influence. He was never a tradition-alist and was full of mischief. He nevertheless always kept his priorities right and helped many others to do the same. The CICCU leadership especially owed a great deal to him.

'The Groups' returned to Cambridge in strength in 1929–32 and became influential with some support from

Deans and Chaplains. They presented a choice between 'orthodoxy and life'. Why cling to orthodoxy if the Groups offered life? But their influence soon waned as the fruits of their work were seen on the whole to be ephemeral. Many people were helped by their challenge; but in those cases where the response lasted and grew into something life-long, it was for the most part among people who had already a good biblical basis for their faith or who maintained a discipline of Bible study and Bible exposition.

In both these ways the CICCU, in fellowship with the other CUs in the IVF, hammered out a policy. Co-operation with bodies that did not have the same witness was increasingly clearly not only unfruitful and inconsistent, it was positively harmful to the clarity and authority of the gospel. The CICCU was not prepared for the gospel to be seen as just one human point of view amongst other more rational and more 'traditional' alternatives. They had to be distinctive and clear, and free to get on with a frankly Bible-based ministry. They had to stand against liberalism on their right and an unbiblical super-spirituality on their left.

Such a policy was not easily maintained. There was constant pressure for the CICCU, the College groups and the CUs in other Universities to treat their doctrinal stance as less important, so that they could join in joint activities and official fellowship. Generation after generation of students had to think it out and decide whether the truths at issue were important enough to necessitate a distinctive witness. The key concept was 'witness'; what do we stand for and what is our public witness? It affected the Membership Basis, Doctrinal Basis for committee members and speakers, and any joint platform with other theologies. Every year there were some who disagreed and put their energies more into the SCM than the CU. But many of those who concluded that they must be distinctive have gone on to be leaders in the church and have been valiant for truth in key positions all round the world.

Chapter Seven

1930 - 1945
The turn of the tide

By 1930 the CICCU was established as a minority group. As we have seen, their theology was laughed at and, while their zeal and sincerity were admired, they were not taken very seriously by most religious or intellectual people. They were regarded as anti-intellectual, anti-theological and obscurantist, clinging tenaciously to outmoded beliefs simply because they were afraid to face the facts. The University was a far more self-consciously intellectual community than it is today. At least, those who were influential in the student world were on the whole more intellectual, particularly in religious and anti-religious circles. Skill in sport was still highly rated, but intellectual ability was, for most people, more important. There were some idle (and usually wealthy) students reading for ordinary degrees and doing as little work as possible, but their numbers were steadily declining.

Cambridge still had much of a glorified boarding-school atmosphere. The majority of students did come from boarding-schools and, of the rest, many were very middle-class. The debating atmosphere of a good sixth form was continued in Cambridge with the addition of the added intellectual confidence given by a few years. As one student put it, 'When I came up to Cambridge, I thought that all intellectual problems were pretty well settled and that our generation knew most of what one needed to know. It took me three years to discover how ignorant I was.' Guests had to be out of College or lodgings by 10 p.m. Unless by special permission, all undergraduates had to be in by midnight. Cap and gown were worn outside College after dark or one was liable to be fined 6s. 8d. by a Proctor. Hospitality was formal. Almost everyone dined in Hall at least five evenings a week (you had to pay for that anyway) and most people sat in approximately the same place night after night with the same group of friends and acquaintances.

In this context, enthusiastic Christianity was frowned upon. CICCU members were regarded as embarrassingly eccentric and their personal evangelism was in rather bad taste. They were at best a curiosity, like those frighteningly clever and hard-working students from provincial grammar schools, who were beginning to win more and more of the College scholarships. To go to Chapel was reasonable, though not many went; but to be an active CICCU member was crazy. The minority of ex-grammar schoolboys were more serious-minded and there were excellent Christians among them; but they rarely took the lead in CICCU, or in other societies, because it took them a year or so to be at home in the rather new and alien atmosphere of this residential community. The ex-grammar schoolboys, however, began to have a healthy broadening influence on the social base and outlook of the CICCU as well as of the rest of the University. During the war the University became distinctively and irreversibly less 'public school' and less Church of England and the CICCU followed suit.

Basil Atkinson

There were practically no senior members of the University who would associate with the CICCU. Of the seniors, Basil Atkinson alone came regularly to DPM and threw his bachelor house open on Tuesday nights for open discussion.[59] 'Basil At.' provided a major influence for a strong doctrinal policy over many years to 1970, when he became a sick man (he died in 1971). In the early '20s he had seemed rather erratic and too dogmatic about what was God's will for the CICCU. Earnshaw Smith had been a wiser and more inspiring adviser. But in the 1930s 'Basil At.' became a much appreciated elder statesman. He did not now try to dictate to the CICCU, he advised. Occasionally he urged a point; generally he prayed privately and exercised his influence by friendship. He had an explosive sense of humour and was himself the subject of endless jokes. Because the CICCU laughed at him, they did not find his influence oppressive and he was greatly respected and loved. Each term he took three or four College Bible studies weekly, so most members benefited from his Bible exposition. He was an excellent Greek scholar, violently against Roman Catholicism and enthusiastic for evangelical truth. His views were sometimes quaint, always sincere. When someone prayed in a prayer meeting for the Pope who was ill, and added that the Pope had done so much good, Basil exploded with a violent 'No'! Many, many students owed their continued doctrinal orthodoxy to his help and prayers. Archdeacon Guillebaud of Ruanda was also at home in Cambridge for part of the period, and his house on Barton Road was a centre of lively discussion and (marvellously and helpfully) a place where the CICCU men and women could meet naturally at least for the huge Sunday buffet lunches that Mrs G. provided.

'Basil At.' and Archdeacon Guillebaud, who was a scholarly Bible translator, provided some real stimulus to deeper Bible study. Christy Innes, an Aberdeen graduate studying at Westminster College (the Presbyterian theological college in Cambridge), and John Wenham helped to get the Theological Students Prayer Union going in Cambridge. The TSPU (now Theological Students' Fellowship) meetings drew theologs and a number of non-theologs. It helped greatly towards a more positive desire to get the best out of theological study and steadied many waverers. Dr R. E. D. Clark, who was a chemistry research student and demonstrator, started with others an apologetics discussion group. This was never quite accepted by the CICCU hierarchy but it helped some to a less anti-intellectual stance. This started back in 1929 with papers by Basil Atkinson and F. D. Coggan (later Archbishop of Canterbury) amongst others, and continued right up until 1940 in a spasmodic way.

Campers

Meanwhile the evangelism went on. A succession of people connected with camps for public schoolboys, especially the 'Bash Camps' (led by 'Bash', *i.e.* the Rev. E. J. H. Nash), sent up to Cambridge a remarkable group of freshers who already had some skill in evangelism. They emphasized the 'simple gospel' and, being trained in work with schoolboys, were sometimes anti-intellectual and anti-theological. That gradually righted itself, however, for most of them as they gained experience. Their ablest men became intellectually and theologically some of the more adventurous and effective evangelists and teachers of the next generation. They were also excellent personal evangelists. At one time it was a joke that to be a member of the University Hockey team it was necessary either to be a CICCU member or to attend CICCU sermons. The reason was that a 'Bash camper' was the Captain of Hockey and brought all the members of the team along to the Sunday night sermons – often trailing in a little late because he (and the Secretary, also a Christian) had been rounding up a straggler.

In the years 1935–39 the four CICCU Presidents were all 'Bash campers' and this created some restlessness, though they were good Presidents. Like all other fellowships-within-a-fellowship, the 'campers' could be a bit overwhelming and they irritated some people of other outlooks and backgrounds by their special emphasis and their concentration on men from the 'best' schools. But the CICCU owed much to them and they were reliable in policy and doctrine. They also brought a fresh concern for the ministry at home as opposed to abroad. Some regarded this as a dangerous diversion from missionary interest, but in fact it supplemented the concern for overseas service rather than competing with it. Many of these men went on to Ridley Hall and helped CICCU College groups in a pastoral capacity, sometimes leading their group Bible studies. Some had a deep influence for good year by year on the young Christians and new converts. This was especially true where they helped humbly and prayerfully and gave them friendship. They also helped the CICCU to be more tactful.

Background factors

At this time, however, the evangelical world was suffering an intellectual inferiority complex. A fresher in 1938 was warned in a friendly way by an older and slightly rebellious CICCU man not to advertise his interest in contemporary poetry, lest he be regarded as unsound. This was not fair, but it had some truth in it.[60] Many were frightened of intellectual activity. The evangelical world generally seemed to be in decline. Many of its ablest young men and women were going liberal or losing their faith at university. In Cambridge it seemed that more were being lost to the cause than were being gained through conversion. In the year 1939–40 a CICCU member calculated that only about a dozen had professed conversion through the CICCU, though in fact there were probably considerably more.

The number of strong evangelical churches in the country was small. Many traditionally evangelical churches had now become liberal. The range of suitable speakers was therefore limited. Brethren influence was still quite strong and a number of the most articulate CICCU members came from that background. They seemed to keep to an orthodox faith in this difficult period better than many of the Anglican majority. But few of the Brethren students, of course, studied theology in the aggressively liberal theological Faculty, and they were also helped by the fact that their tradition was, in any case, staunchly independent of prevailing religious opinions. Very few students came up from the smaller independent churches that nowadays supply some fine leadership. CICCU was mainly Church of England or Brethren with a mere handful of others.

The University as a whole was cynical about religion. Life was easy-going. The undergraduates believed that they comprised an élite and they were correspondingly conceited and self-satisfied. Hitler's doings on the Continent were shocking but far away. The student body in general was apathetic about religion and did not wish to discuss its verities. Probably the situation has never been quite so difficult again. Yet men and women were won for Christ in a steady flow and a growing number entered the ministry.

In June 1939 Cambridge was the venue for a great international conference convened by the IVF and its overseas associated movements which have now formed the International Fellowship of Evangelical Students. The Scandinavians chartered a ship and brought six hundred or so over. The CICCU provided numerous guides and some of the organizers. Many of its members were made aware of the international scene in a new way and in the following years played an active part in the IFES. But the clouds of war were gathering quickly. Some of those who came from the Continent warned others that war was inevitable. They realized that very shortly not a few conference members were likely to be killed. It was, of course, only two months before the war began.

Munich and the Second World War

The Munich crisis had come just before term began in 1938 and during the following year the increasing likelihood of war had begun to be realized even in the University.

Conscientious objectors, including some of the CICCU men, began to face tribunals. They were supported by Basil Atkinson, who had been imprisoned in the First World War as a conscientious objector. Student life, however, did not change until the war began in 1939. Then immediately courses were shortened and call-up began in earnest. Throughout the Second World War the University continued in considerable strength. Military units were quartered in parts of some Colleges and six-month courses began for Forces' cadets. These latter were fully part of the University and effective work was done among them. Freshers' squashes had to be held twice a year, some at Easter and others in October as usual. Evangelistic work began to be more fruitful. Perhaps life was more serious than in the cynical 1930s. The CICCU became smaller but more compact. At about 150 members (it had 230 official members in 1937 and 130 in 1943–1944), the committee knew all of them at least by sight. And God worked. A remarkable freshers' sermon in 1941 saw about twenty professions of conversion. This was a new phenomenon for the CICCU and a number of those converted then are now well known in the Christian world. A rather raw Forces' cadet straight from school came up for an Air Force course. He joined the Air Force because he could think of nothing better than to be killed soon. If he was going to die soon, he might as well do it with zest. He was converted through Derek Podmore, another Forces' cadet, an ordinand in the CICCU. When Podmore was killed in action the new convert, who survived, went on to a fruitful ministry in the Church of England. There were quite a few like him.

Several London Colleges were evacuated to Cambridge for the duration of the war. The London School of Economics Christian Union, which had died out, was restarted with CICCU help and met in a member's College room for some time. Bedford College, Bart's Hospital Medical School and part of University College, London, all had flourishing CUs before long, making good use of the CICCU sermons and Bible readings and seeing not a few professions of conversion.

It was not a promising time for new developments and yet certain important new trends set in. A very capable group of men were up studying theology, led by the older than usual President of 1942.[61] A high percentage of first-class degrees in theology went to CICCU men in the next few years. This gave a new confidence and the old, rather defensive attitudes began to give way to a more confident and even aggressive theological outlook. Men were being won over from a liberal to a conservative theology. Some of the most hostile teachers of theology began to change their tone. Tyndale House was bought by the IVF in 1942 to be a centre of biblical research in Cambridge. It became a place where there were nearly always some capable post-graduates of theological acumen available for consultation. Tyndale House bears witness to two things. First, it was the fruit of the conviction that theology was now so liberal that men of conservative convictions had little chance of getting accepted for research in most Universities. Evangelical research was needed to recapture the field, but it would have to be outside the University system. Secondly, Tyndale House was sited in Cambridge because there the old tradition of more objective biblical scholarship was still as strong as anywhere in the United Kingdom. The Faculty was liberal but willing to give a first-class degree to any man who was good. They were also willing to help men to do really scholarly textual study, though they might not help them to get research grants if they were conservative. Research students were also being pushed into work on the most 'dry' topics – far removed from biblical studies or doctrinal studies.

During the war another group of research students in the CICCU and some older undergraduates began to meet to discuss apologetic questions, especially questions on science and faith. They discovered that they could do at least as well at this kind of activity as the more liberal groups and, encouraged by the IVF, a first conference for the Research Scientists' Christian Fellowship was called by some CICCU men (including R. E. D. Clark) and met in Cambridge.

Growth and development

In other ways also the tide began to turn. The CICCU, in spite of the youth of its members, when few were up for more than two years, became rather more adventurous. Some apologetics lectures, begun as an experiment, did not come off, however, because of the lack of experience. But at least they tried. The SCM was now weak among undergraduates and the CICCU was becoming a little more mature and less shrill. The Chapels and the SCM, with their overwhelming senior support, still provided a strong alternative. The Methodist Society became the largest religious body in Cambridge and ran a series of group meetings that some CICCU members found more attractive than the CICCU College Bible studies. The latter were still largely monologues by Basil Atkinson, or one of the Ridley men. But towards the end of this period experiments were being carried out in the Colleges with a discussion style of Bible study. Before long this became a general pattern, with perhaps one term in three devoted to a series of Bible readings given by Basil Atkinson or someone else. The change was helpful and led to a more active searching of the Scriptures by the ordinary member for himself. IVF books had begun to appear. Archdeacon Guillebaud and G. T. Manley (now in a parish) produced the first edition of *Search the Scriptures* (1934–37) with the CICCU partly in mind. Although it was not devotional enough for some and never caught on universally in the CICCU, it helped many to go deeper than the rather superficial devotional guides that they had been using. *In understanding be men* (a handbook on Christian doctrine) and other Inter-Varsity Press books began to supply the need for doctrine and apologetics and provided some important help in the field of evangelical literature at a student level.

John Stott was a student from 1940 to 1945 and already showed unusual gifts. The CICCU Exec., however, had the sense to send one of their number to tell him that they would not invite him to join the next committee as they believed he should be free from committee meetings. They wanted him to get on with the evangelistic and pastoral work in which he was exercising an outstanding ministry. As the Exec. met for a whole evening and a substantial time of prayer on Sunday morning each week, as well as involving members in a range of other obligations, this was a sensible policy. It illustrates the fact that the real work of the CICCU was often not carried out by officials or committees. The whole effectiveness of the CICCU depended on the fact that a high proportion of ordinary members, both then and in almost all periods of its history, were active in personal evangelism and in helping one another in every way. The committee were very much looked up to and their example was influential; but they were not the CICCU, and the tone of each College group was the major influence.

At this time the Sunday morning Bible reading was changed to Saturday night, and this gave the speaker much greater scope. In any case, Sunday mornings always tempted people to skip church and to come straight from an early morning Chapel Communion and a time of personal quiet to the Bible reading at 12.30. Now more people went to local churches on Sunday mornings and the Saturday night speakers had a longer time in which to speak. The great evangelistic opportunity was the Sunday night sermon. When the blackout was enforced and Holy Trinity was for a while no longer available, there was anxiety as to what to do. The only suitable blacked-out hall was the Dorothy Café ballroom, and that was very expensive. As the Exec.

were discussing it, the Secretary returned to his room to find on his desk an anonymous gift from a student of cash for the right amount for one week's rent. They booked the ballroom and continued there until Holy Trinity was available again, money coming in as needed. Many continued to be converted in a steady, though not spectacular, stream and the members learnt biblical truth and life in a warm fellowship of active witness which contrasted sharply with the formality and coldness of most of the Chapels and the more intellectual, but usually spiritually sterile, debates at the SCM. The 'Meth. Soc.' and the Baptist Society ('The Robert Hall Society') stood between the two, providing a mixed diet of biblical and liberal speakers and activities. Holy Trinity Church had very few strongly biblical preachers and the CICCU stalwarts went increasingly to St Paul's Church. It was not until late in the war that the 'Round Church' began also to attract evangelical students (it gradually took over from the rather more distant St Paul's as the main CICCU church in the late '50s). By the seventies there was a far wider choice of biblical ministry and CICCU members were widely distributed in the churches in Cambridge.

Whether people were clever or athletic did not matter so much any more. Life was too short. It mattered only that people were genuine and the CICCU provided a transparently sincere fellowship in evangelism and Bible study. Friendships were strong and lasting. New converts were drawn into a lively and warm community for a while and then scattered to the battle-fields and war-time research establishments of the world. A prayer fellowship for ex-members in the Forces was strong and, with the CICCU ex-members list, this helped to form part of the nucleus of the Graduates' Fellowship of the IVF which was created in 1941. In 1941 and 1942 the IVF annual conference was held in Cambridge and more CICCU members than usual attended, with considerable benefit to the CICCU. These gatherings had the affect also of making senior members of the University treat the CICCU more seriously.

In a difficult time the CICCU members seemed to have a spiritual vitality that was not common. They had a faith which was adequate to the prospect of death and it was a faith to live by. A number of people were helped by the question that, in any case, posed itself in the occasional air-raid: 'Am I ready to die, and what is my confidence if I am called to stand before God tonight?' One fresher at least came back, after a CICCU Sunday sermon and a personal talk, saying to his friend the next day, 'Yes, I am trusting Christ for my forgiveness. I am ready to die in an air-raid tonight.' Of those who bothered to attend College Chapel, a growing percentage turned out to be CICCU members. But the Chapel fraternity was a distinct group as a rule, with not too much overlap. CICCU people attended Chapel, because it was the official religion, as a public witness and in order to get to know other people who might be looking for a vital faith and whom CICCU, therefore, might be able to help. They did not often attend the other activities of the Chapel group regularly. The majority of members were total abstainers from alcohol and rarely went to the cinema or the theatre. At the time these were, of course, the traditions of the evangelical churches and the youth movements, such as Crusaders, which sent up each year a strong contingent of Christian freshers. The Chaplains' traditional hospitality was a sherry party and the CICCU tended to avoid this and even the Chapel breakfast after Communion, because it could interfere with the Quiet Time.

The Doctrinal Basis
Cambridge, however, remained curiously remote from the war and was bombed only slightly on two or three occasions. Everyone was busy with trying to keep things going on the reduced scale that alone was possible. The CICCU members

113

were inevitably younger and some College groups were led by very recent converts. It was decided, therefore, that the College reps must be asked to agree a short doctrinal statement if they were not be at the mercy of liberal or High-Church influence. Yet some of the people in view were so young in the faith that their signature of the whole Doctrinal Basis could not be a carefully thought-out agreement. In the end it was agreed to ask the College reps to sign that 'in accepting the responsibilities of membership of the General Committee, I agree to recognize the doctrinal basis of the IVFEU as being the standard of doctrine and as determining the policy of the General Committee of the CICCU: and I will undertake to support only such matters as are fully consistent with it.' This worked well and prevented the College groups from inviting unsuitable speakers and from being over-influenced by powerful personalities of another view.

The policy issues were clear. As a war-time Exec. memorandum stated, 'our attitude therefore to doctrines contrary to Scripture cannot be one of approval or toleration. We have got to say boldly that they are false as judged, not by our own opinion, but by the objective standards of Scripture. There is therefore a fundamental divergence of belief with a number of Christian bodies. Some deny the final authority of Scripture implicitly by saying that every "point of view" is good . . . to co-operate with such bodies is ourselves implicitly to deny the final authority of Scripture . . .'

This had to be constantly argued out because of the constant pressure for co-operation from Chaplains and above all the SCM. It seemed a tiresome and time-wasting occupation to go over the issues again and again; yet those who were forced to think it out became some of the most reliable and consistent evangelical Christians in their future life and work.

Defence and proclamation

The CICCU had learnt to call heresy by its name and on the whole they did so not ungraciously. They believed themselves to be set for the defence and proclamation of the gospel. They ran a Mission every three years, though these were not, at this stage, very fruitful efforts. There seemed to be no really suitable missioners available and the painstaking personal evangelism of the members and the Sunday sermons were more fruitful than the Missions. Each Mission, however, did reach a number who probably would not otherwise have heard the gospel. On the other hand a very big Mission and the other activities run by the SCM seemed to achieve very little indeed, for the message was not clear or biblical. Gradually the CICCU began to be a major religious force in the undergraduate world once again. Though very few people could see it at the time, the tide had turned; not because the CICCU was better or stronger, but because the alternatives to a biblical Christianity were being tried and found wanting in the fires of war and its aftermath. People, once again, were very willing to listen to an old-fashioned biblical message. The theological Faculty of the time would have laughed at the suggestion. They were quite sure that only a liberal/rationalistic approach could help the modern man. The official representatives of religion mostly wrote the CICCU off as schoolboy religion which would fade out in due time. But not many were so hotly antagonistic as before. The more ecumenical spirit was against opposing anything. On the other hand these seniors were not in fact as likely to have a basic sympathy with evangelical religion as in the 1920s. At the undergraduate level, however, the CICCU was rapidly gaining ground and getting a much better hearing. Whatever the seniors said, the undergraduate with a spiritual need or with an awakened conscience tended to turn much more often to the CICCU and try to understand what they were saying.

The life of a CICCU member

The active CICCU member's Christian life had, at this period, three main focal points, The Quiet Time was widely observed. Probably almost everyone set aside at least twenty minutes, some an hour or more, for personal prayer and Bible study every day. There was considerable emphasis on this, both officially and unofficially.

Secondly, the College group was, in contrast with earlier times, the focus of fellowship. In 1937 these groups ranged from twenty-five to two in actual membership. But some non-members and a few non-Christians came regularly to the Bible studies. In every College there was a weekly Bible study and also a weekly prayer meeting attended by the majority of the actual members. Some of the College groups had breakfast together once a week before the prayer meeting. The College rep.'s task was overwhelmingly pastoral and a good rep. would get round his members, have prayer with them and encourage them in evangelism and in the Christian life. The lines were drawn very tightly on the question of amusement (drink, dancing, theatre and cinema). But as one non-Christian observer remarked, 'The CICCU seems to be the best social club in the university.' What he meant was that it drew in people of all Faculties and types (although there were no women members) in a fellowship that was transparently genuine. The friendships were formed mostly on a College basis (sometimes on a Faculty basis, especially in medicine and science). There was much mutual challenge to go all out and win others for Christ. Among the more active, anyone who did not have a friend to bring to a Sunday sermon felt something of a failure. These friends were prayed for by name in College prayer meetings. The pressure to bring someone to sermons was probably sometimes overdone and a more natural witness could probably have been as effective and less stressful, but they were deeply in earnest and the quieter and less activist members found a natural and positive role within the fellowship.

Thirdly, beyond the College circle, many members went to central activities. A fairly high proportion went to DPM once or twice a week. Third-year members often took freshers under their wing and introduced them to the various central activities, such as the DPM and the week-end Bible reading and the Saturday night PM which focused on the Sunday sermon. That included many personal prayers for non-Christians, and was a stirring experience, with Basil Atkinson's urgent, and sometimes quaint, prayers which encouraged others to pray aloud, even if they could not express themselves in elegant language.

The week-end Bible reading was a school of Christian teaching such as was rarely available in churches or any-where else. Many members learnt far more than they realized at the time from this weekly exercise. The Sunday night evangelistic sermons also helped to form a clear idea of the gospel. The great opportunity of personal talks afterwards was a practical school of evangelism and the means of con-version for many.

Work was taken seriously by the Christians on the whole and a certain amount of Christian reading was fairly widely encouraged and practised. There were still some who did as little work as possible so as to be free for evangelism (and sport). Some regarded this as the best training for missionary or pastoral ministry. But as life became more serious, concern to do well at work also became more general. Speakers such as Professor Rendle Short from less ivory-tower Universities helped here and deliberately made this point from time to time. But as has always been the case in a residential University, an enormous amount of time was spent, much of it profitably, in personal discussion and debate with both Christians and non-Christians. The CICCU was not cliquish. Nearly all the members had quite a few non-Christian friends. But the close friendships were nearly all within the circle of other CICCU members.

Social concern

In the early 1920s the lines between the CICCU and the SCM had been definite but not so tightly drawn as to prevent some of the leaders from holding office in both societies (*e.g.* Stephen Neill and Max Warren, who were both to become international missionary statesmen). As the SCM became more clearly the voice of liberal theology, this became impossible. In this there were some important gains. The witness of the CICCU and its leaders became clearer doctrinally. That was essential to evangelism, because the biblical gospel needed to be sharply contrasted with the liberal gospel. But at the same time, the CICCU men could become too isolated and their faith a little brittle as a result. They might never meet and debate with others while at Cambridge, but they were sure to have to do so when they went down, and some were not well prepared for that. There was also on both sides a danger of over-reaction against a caricature of the other. After a while the CICCU leaders began to take the initiative in making personal contact with SCM leaders, and that helped.

The question of social involvement was probably the outstanding example. The SCM spent a lot of its energy in discussing social questions. This had been one of the differences between them and the CICCU way back in 1910, although it had not been the major question of debate. Now it loomed bigger. Was social concern in the SCM a cause or a symptom of its weakness on the gospel? It had started in the SCM as a desire to apply the Bible to social questions; by 1935 what SCM was doing was open to criticism as being neither well based on the Bible nor dealing with real questions for the student. It also distracted them from evangelism. The SCM was led by older men who tried to run its programme as if it was a ministers' fraternal. Even the strong influence of William Temple in the Central Councils of the SCM meant that it was often talking about questions that were quite outside the experience of students.

In 1933 Basil Atkinson re-edited *Old Paths in Perilous Times* (see p.78) and copies were given free to all CICCU freshers for a while. A comparatively mild statement in the first edition was reprinted in the second edition: 'no amount of reform will raise a man one degree from spiritual blindness and degradation; it may even make harder the humiliation involved in accepting Christianity. The plan which God has ordained is regeneration.' But in the second edition there was added a new paragraph: 'While believing that it is always a part of Christian duty to ameliorate distress, the CICCU cannot be enthusiastic about schemes for bringing world peace by means of political bodies such as the League of Nations, or social uplift by methods of reform. It holds that in the Gospel of Christ alone lies the only hope for the world by the regeneration of the individual. All else consists merely of "dead works" without permanent value before God and may be written down as "vanity".' That was a more hard-line position – it was actually negative about social work.

When asked what was the difference between CICCU and SCM, a common reply was to the effect that, while the SCM concerned itself with the social application of Christianity, the CICCU concerned itself with Christianity itself – a personal relationship to God. As a statement of fact this was true, though it was not the whole story and perhaps it was not the best way of explaining things. In this, however, the CICCU reflected the evangelicalism of the period. At a time when few nominal Christians knew the gospel, concern with social questions seemed a fatal distraction from the main job in hand, and CICCU leaders thought that they could see that social concern had led the SCM into spiritual ineffectiveness. The CICCU over-reacted to the SCM as did evangelicals generally. The questions to be asked should have been, first, is such concern biblical and second, what sort of priority does it have?

It is interesting, however, that some of the leaders in a

more positive evangelical attitude to social questions in Britain came from this period in the CICCU. Sir Norman Anderson, for instance, was President in 1930–31 and Sir Frederick Catherwood was Vice-President in 1944. There are others also.[62] They may not have had that attitude to social questions while they were students, but once free of the need to take a stand over against the SCM it was easier to ask in a more open way what the teaching of the Bible really does imply for social questions. Since 1945, as the SCM has weakened, a more positive attitude has ruled. The CICCU, however, has always had a problem of priorities, as does the church at large. While the CICCU was (and still is) preoccupied with evangelism and the nurture of new Christians who know almost nothing about the Bible, social concern always seemed a remote luxury. That is a different approach to the problem from the hard-line quotation from *Old Paths* given above. The CICCU has increasingly seen social concern as right but needing to be left very largely until one is in the more real world of employment and the wider community where the problems and opportunities are no longer armchair questions. It has never been more than a very small number of members who have felt, while still students, that these questions had high priority. Nevertheless by 1970 it was perfectly natural for some members to go to specialized conferences (mainly of graduates) where these concerns were being discussed. In the 1930s it might have been looked at not only as a dangerous diversion from the task in hand but, in terms of the quotation given, as an unbiblical thing to be doing.

Before 1946 many CICCU members, when they left Cambridge, weakened their basic evangelical convictions if they got into social questions. The two had seemed incompatible and some of the liberal leaders in Cambridge frequently said to CICCU men, 'The CICCU is fine to get you converted; but if you want to live in the real world you must go on to another theology.' After 1946 this was no longer so persuasive. That was partly because the CICCU members were then for a while older and many members were as experienced in life as those who said this, and partly because already during the late '30s and early '40s the foundation had begun to be laid for a more plainly biblical theology that was not so dominated by reactions against anything. It was now easier to ask: What does the Bible say and what are its applications to any and every sphere of life? There is as yet no evangelical consensus, but the approach is more healthy.

Chapter Eight

1945 – 1955
The renewed evangelicalism

When the war finished and the ex-servicemen came back, they provided a more mature community. Not a few were married. The sight of undergraduates pushing prams was greeted with astonishment by those who had known the University in the '30s. During the war, when an Exec. member became engaged (to a member of one of the London University CUs evacuated to Cambridge for the war), some people had assumed he would resign from the committee because he had set an undesirable example! The public-school attitude to women had predominated and the CICCU men held aloof and often rudely ignored women whom they knew in the CU when they met elsewhere in public. A war-time Exec., after spending a total of twenty-four hours discussing possible amalgamation of the CICCU with the CWICCU, had decided that, even though it was probably desirable, the male membership did not want it and it should wait until they did. The post-war generation amalgamated the two Unions with hardly a ripple of dissent in 1948.

Evangelism was direct and outreach widespread. Undergraduates knew what evil was. Many were aware of sin in their lives, and interest in the gospel was much easier to arouse than it had been before the war. Schoolboy philosophies had been shattered in the Forces. The CICCU seized the opportunity with enthusiasm. The official religious establishment was strong and many of the College Chaplains were very able people. College Chapels were well attended again and not all the CICCU men saw the need to give a distinctively biblical witness. Nevertheless the initiative went increasingly to men whose Christian life had stood the test of time in the Forces. On the whole that meant men whose lives had been fed on personal prayer and Bible reading. The leaders in Chapel groups were therefore often sympathetic to the CICCU, if they were not actually members. The CICCU grew in size and effectiveness.

Some of the new leaders had been in Cambridge for part of a course before or during the war. The old spiritual emphases were maintained. Besides, the ex-service leaders were men of action and were prepared to stand up to anyone, however academically respectable, without fear. The CICCU lost its slight inferiority complex. The theology lecturers and College tutors were, after all, not so much older and they often knew less of life than the students. Tyndale House was a help and men continued to get good theological degrees in fair numbers. The DPM and Saturday night Bible reading were growing.

The number of overseas students in Cambridge increased greatly after the war and for the first time the CICCU began to do a more adequate job in welcoming and helping them. It was never more than a small group who were greatly involved with this work and there is bound to be some regret that so few were active. The overseas students of that generation have become extremely influential leaders in many countries. Happily there were a number of outstanding Christians among them who owe at least something to the friendship and witness of the CICCU. In the Billy Graham Mission (1955) it needed a persistent assistant missioner to persuade the CICCU to organize, at short notice, a meeting in Trinity Old Combination Room at which Dr Graham himself would speak. The CICCU thought very few would come, but over 120 turned up and the meeting had to be moved to the dining-hall, for which urgent and rather irregular permission was gained at the last moment. Many were deeply impressed.

The co-operation question again

In 1946 all the Christian groups in the University were invited to join in a new unity under a body called 'Koinonia'.[63] At first the CICCU was involved, but they soon discovered how superficial the unity was. A widespread and spontaneous feeling developed that 'the impetus of such an effort would be slight in view of the loose doctrinal basis and the varied devotional standards of its supporters'. By April 1946 the CICCU decided to plan their own Mission for February '47 and were as certain as their predecessors that 'unity in doctrine is essential as a basis for evangelism'. So the CICCU withdrew from Koinonia, but agreed that the Mission should coincide with the Koinonia Mission. The latter had an able and well-known speaker, Alec Vidler. The CICCU, following the pattern of several not very effective previous Missions, had a team of three, each to speak for two or three nights. It did not look very promising and a number of the CICCU leaders were really uncertain as to whether these plans were right.

In July a small CICCU party at Keswick, including the President, heard the dramatic and effective preaching of Dr Donald Grey Barnhouse from USA. They decided to ask him to come and be their missioner. He could not manage February 1947, but offered November '46 instead. After prayer the CICCU President accepted and returned to his lodgings to find a letter from Koinonia to say that they were forced to alter the date of their Mission also – by one week. The CICCU therefore, to the relief of many, went on alone again. February '47, when the Koinonia Mission was held, also proved in the event to be one of the coldest months on record and with a fuel shortage to match it was an unfortunate month for a mission. November '46 proved far better.

The great Missions

This Mission was well planned. War-time administrative experience was useful and, in spite of bread rationing, over a hundred smaller tea meetings (squashes) were planned for the week. A substantial team of associate missioners was employed for the first time and they were kept constantly busy. Barnhouse preached in Great St Mary's (because Holy Trinity Church was too small) to packed audiences – probably rarely less than 800. Many doubters and many frank unbelievers came and heard a lively, well-illustrated and authoritative message from the Bible. Many will remember his dramatic description of himself as a child trying to lift himself off the ground by his own bootlaces – a comparison with justification by works.

A young atheist, for instance, was brought along. She was one of the leaders of the University Communist Party, but was converted and subsequently became a missionary in Japan. Her interest had first been aroused by the life of a Christian friend. As so often it was primarily Christian friendship which persuaded people to come and hear the gospel. There were many other converts, some of them prominent today in Christian work.

Barnhouse was also exceedingly dogmatic. He did not have an after-meeting, but nevertheless preached for decision. He was scathing about contemporary theology and provoked the theological Faculty to anger. One of his addresses to theological students was based on Malachi 2 in terms that were crude and far from calculated to win friends ('I will spread dung upon your faces'). He was witty, pugnacious and sincere, very good in the numerous personal interviews which he had. When he left over a hundred had professed conversion, many had been stirred up to seek further and the CICCU had finally abandoned all hesitation.

It stood in a new way as an aggressively evangelical body in doctrine and in evangelism.

The CICCU grew. Some College groups were up to thirty strong. The weekly College Bible study and prayer meeting were well attended. The united Saturday night Bible reading had to be moved from the Henry Martyn Hall to a bigger hall and again, in 1951, to the debating chamber of the Union. It drew up to 350, occasionally more. It was probably the largest meeting of any kind in Cambridge on a Saturday night (the University had at that time about 8,000 members). The DPM swelled and on Sundays drew 140 or more. There was no room to kneel and not time for all to take part. Prayers were brief and precise and finished with a resounding 'Amen'. There were nearly 600 at the Sunday sermon as a rule, perhaps one third of them non-Christians.

In 1949 Barnhouse came for a second Mission. Once more there were a good many striking conversions, once more there was controversy and antagonism. Barnhouse was merciless with other views including, in CICCU circles, those who did not share his pre-millennial view of the second coming. Those who felt his lash did not usually like it. But, if he was rough, it was a language which the ex-service undergraduates understood, even if the more smooth seniors thought it bad taste. Almost all the male students had either done war service or a two-year national service.

In November 1952 the Mission was led by John Stott. Until 1950 he had been a curate in a London parish and he was still in his early thirties, though now Rector of All Souls' Church in London. He had been a leading member of the CICCU during the war and he understood the Cambridge scene. He was biblical, scholarly though not academic, firm though not caustic, more evidently a man with love for people than some of the older preachers. The impact was perhaps broader than any Mission since 1900.

Ten years later Basil Atkinson wrote of this, 'I judge it to be the highest point of those wonderful nine years (1946-55), the nearest to revival that we have yet reached.' A very large number professed faith in Christ. The liberals began to comment on John Stott as a new phenomenon in evangelicalism and to be aware that the CICCU was not to be ignored in theology, apologetics or thoughtful evangelism. In fact the phenomenon was not new. John Stott represented the best of the CICCU tradition. The only new thing was that he was one of the younger men who had got as much as possible out of doing a modern theology course (getting a 'first'). He could speak to the theologs and others with sympathy as well as with biblical authority. His addresses formed the basis of the book *Basic Christianity*.[64] Christianity was presented as inescapably true both in theory and in practice and the lives of the CICCU and their works had to back it up. The focus was on the Person and work of Christ. Cambridge was still at that time a community that gave a good deal of respect to Christian morality. Theology was in confusion but, as the liberals often said, 'We all believe in the Christian life and the Sermon on the Mount.' They went on, wrongly, to conclude that what we believed didn't therefore matter much. It was only later that it was seen that the new theology led to the new morality. A missioner could therefore still rely on a certain awareness of sin and a good deal more biblical knowledge than would be true twenty-five years later. The CICCU stood alone for totally free forgiveness through the death of the divine Christ as our Substitute. Evangelism focused on these truths. Many students came up to Cambridge with some knowledge of 'the law of God'; very few of them really knew the gospel until they heard it in Cambridge.

Why Missions?

This may be the right point at which to ask why Missions have played such a big part in the history of the CICCU.

There seem to be two main reasons. First, Missions gave a unique opportunity of presenting the whole Christian message on the authority of God. In Universities the tendency is to regard religious views as just human opinion open to debate and discussion and having no authority other than the transient authority of the current academic fashion. The sermons, and especially the Missions, gave the opportunity to say clearly that God has spoken and to outline what He has said. There was a place for discussion to lead up to a Mission or to persuade people to come to hear preaching. There was a place for it to follow up a Mission afterwards. But the CICCU believed that, unless there is an authoritative declaration of the message as a word from God, we fail our listeners. The Missions focused this concern and made it plain that the CICCU had a message to declare.

Secondly, in the relatively circumscribed community of the University (Cambridge was not very large – even in 1977 there are only 11,300 students) a Mission can catch the ear of a large percentage of the University. Publicity, especially personal invitations, creates the situation where a large proportion of the student body can be talking about the theme of the Mission and it becomes easy to invite people to come and hear for themselves.

Missions have been of enormous importance in the relatively residential community of Cambridge. They have played a similar part in student evangelism in many other countries. Of course Missions have sometimes been looked to in the wrong way; CU members have expected them to be a sort of automatic machine that produces converts. When this has been the case, the result has been unfortunate. But if Missions are looked to as a means of sowing rather than reaping – of reaching the normally unreached – then there is a logic in holding one every three years, as the CICCU has done for so long. In this way it is hoped that at least once in his time in Cambridge every student would have as good an opportunity as possible of hearing the gospel, even if he had no Christian friends. God has mightily blessed these efforts over the years and a group of big Missions in this period were in their own way each a major step forward in the evangelistic outreach of the CICCU.

Billy Graham

In 1954, while Billy Graham was conducting his first big crusade in Britain at Harringay, it was suggested that he should come to Cambridge. One of the week-end speakers (Fred H. Crittenden) offered to stand down if Graham could come just for the sermon and he agreed. Over tea with the President some remarks by Graham about the nature of the University provoked Fred Crittenden into saying that he hoped Dr Graham would preach just a simple, direct gospel address and not try to pander to the intellectual debating interests of the students. The President agreed. Graham was surprised and rose from the table saying that in that case he must revise what he was going to say. The service proved fruitful in conversions and also in encouraging Billy Graham to emphasize direct evangelism in his student addresses. He was impressed that the Cambridge students had been willing to listen to that sort of address and had not needed academic argument.

In 1955 Billy Graham came over specially from the USA for the CICCU Mission, bringing only one or two American friends with him. He was supported by John Stott and a very large team of assistant missioners. Great St Mary's was used again, as Holy Trinity was too small, and an overflow relay was arranged in Holy Trinity. Relays by land-line were also arranged to other University CUs. Very large numbers attended. There was extensive counselling of enquirers, including not a few dons and research students, and large numbers professed conversion. So extensive was the response that follow-up proved difficult. Many continued to attend Great St Mary's. A regular meeting was started by Christian dons for those seniors who had been helped. The College

Chaplains were busy in helping those interested and many who professed conversion were weaned from the evangelical tradition by active encouragement to go in another direction.

In 1958 John Stott came again for a Mission under the title, 'What think ye of Christ?' Every College had its own assistant missioner and the CICCU gathered together on the team a really remarkable group of young evangelical ministers and laymen. Such a team could not have been found ten years before. Many of them were the fruits of the evangelism and teaching in the CICCU and OICCU during the previous fifteen years. They brought to light one important side-effect of the evangelistic preaching and the Missions of these years. A growing number of students had received a call to the ministry and a major factor in this had been that they had been given a new vision for a preaching ministry. In this the examples of John Stott and Dr Martyn Lloyd-Jones in London had probably played a key part. The ministry was seen in a new way as an opportunity to preach the Word of God with the authority of God. Evangelical theological colleges, especially in the Church of England, had begun to fill up again and to expand with numerous young graduates, including not a few who had been converted in the CICCU and the OICCU since the war. Churches long in the hands of those with other outlooks began to be recaptured for a more biblical ministry. The Principal of Ridley Hall (a liberal evangelical) lamented that the impetus had gone out of the liberal evangelical tradition and that nearly all the men coming to Ridley were now from a conservative evangelical background with experience in the evangelical youth movements or in the University CUs. No-one could really doubt that the evangelical movement was gaining ground fairly rapidly and this was obviously so as far as Cambridge was concerned.

The IVF and IFES

There continued to be a fairly strong link with IVF. In 1946, for instance, a new CU with six freshers was started in Leicester University College (now Leicester University). The CICCU sent a team for a long week-end and helped to launch the CU into a much more wide-ranging witness in the whole of the University. Teams were sent by arrangement with IVF to several other Universities for evangelistic outreach. The CICCU also provided a good many key members of the IVF national (student) Executive Committee, including a high proportion of its Missionary Secretaries and its Chairmen in the years 1945–55. Two Oxford and two Cambridge men went together, after they had graduated, to New England to help the IVCF of USA in that area for one year. A considerable number of young graduates took teaching posts in African Universities and grammar schools where University education was developing very fast. They helped to start both the Scripture Union groups in schools and the Christian Union work in Universities and Colleges. A Barnhouse Mission convert, Nigel Sylvester, became the leader of the Scripture Union work in Africa. When he came home his place was taken by John Dean, who had been converted at the CICCU freshers' sermon in 1950. The Indian IVF (Union of Evangelical Students of India) was started by an Indian professor and a former CICCU man (David C. C. Watson) getting together to run Bible studies in the Colleges and a Sunday night evening meeting in a church (echoes of the CICCU). It was remarkable that the new evangelical student movements emerging all round the world and joining up with the International Fellowship of Evangelical Students often had a Membership Basis that was essentially, though in their own language, 'I declare my faith in Jesus Christ as my Saviour, my Lord and my God.' An old CICCU man, David Adeney, who had helped to start the Chinese IVF, became the Associate General Secretary of IFES for the Far East and exerted a great influence for the spread of the work in that area.

The Cambridge Seventy

During most of this period missionary interest was at a rather low ebb. In 1951, however, Basil Atkinson spoke at a Missionary Breakfast on the missionary tradition of the CICCU. He mentioned that at one time about forty out of a total membership of a hundred members had gone abroad. Someone asked how many were committed to foreign service today. The Missionary Secretary answered that at present there were only sixteen. This was at a time when the CICCU membership was nearly four hundred. An ex-service freshman in the meeting, John Wheatley-Price, writes, 'That disturbed me deeply,' and it drove him to prayer. In 1954–55 he became Missionary Secretary and some time shortly before that he felt challenged that God was calling the CICCU to pray not for a Cambridge Seven but for a Cambridge Seventy. He and others were suspicious of this sort of thing, but gradually the idea took root. The challenge was presented to the CICCU in the spring term of 1955 and during the following year an informal roll was kept of those who committed themselves to foreign missionary service. The prayer was 'That seventy of our generation in the CICCU should serve the Lord overseas'. Some pledged themselves to go who in fact have never yet gone, and some of them joined in the prayer letter which was circulated for many years but never committed themselves to going. In the end over sixty and probably, in fact, almost if not quite seventy did go abroad. Missionary prayer groups were also developed again and were active still in 1977.

It cannot be said that this constituted a missionary revival, but it was a substantial proportion of that generation of CICCU men to go abroad, particularly when there was such a strong call to the home ministry as well. The Seventy also provided everyone with a challenge to self-sacrificing service.

The College Chapels

The CICCU had learnt the necessity of being distinct from the College Chapels.[65] The preliminaries of the Billy Graham Mission provoked an interesting and not unrepresentative conflict with them. The CICCU had as usual gone ahead and appointed College assistant missioners without consultation with the religious authorities. The latter, however, found themselves in a new and slightly difficult position. For the first time the CICCU was at least as large and probably more influential at the undergraduate level than were the Chapels. Although the CICCU had been firm and gracious, the Chaplains naturally wanted to be in on what they could see would be the major Christian activity of the year. The Deans and Chaplains, who had a regular meeting in which there were only a very few really sympathetic to the CICCU, started a correspondence with the CICCU Exec. over the question of follow-up of the forthcoming mission. In one letter they wrote that they had obtained the agreement of the Bishop of Ely for Billy Graham (a Baptist) to preach in Great St Mary's on the condition that all names of converts were given to the College Chaplains. This was totally unacceptable to the CICCU and there was thought of moving the Mission to some other more neutral meeting-place, if one could be found at short notice. The Deans and Chaplains were warned by the sympathetic few in their numbers that they had made an almost impossible demand. The CICCU Exec. consulted friends in the IVF and elsewhere, who all advised standing firm. While they tried to work out an answer, the correspondence with the Chaplains continued on other topics. After a while the CICCU replied that they noted that the question of converts' names had now been dropped. They hoped it could be forgotten. To associate the CICCU so closely with the Chaplains in this way, they said, would imply a degree of unity in doctrine that neither the CICCU nor the Chaplains really wished to maintain. The subject was never raised again. The Mission was held in Great St Mary's, and the CICCU did not give names to the Chaplains!

Probably the CICCU has never been stronger than it was in this period. The membership, which rose to 400, consisted of students who for the most part understood what the CICCU was for and why it gave a distinctive witness. Many who had been converted in Cambridge continued afterwards in effective Christian witness. The CICCU was not as large as it has sometimes been since, but it was more clearly defined as a biblical group than it has sometimes become when it has been much larger. The rediscovery of evangelical truth as the power of God for conversion and for spiritual life was fresh and exciting. Of course for each generation it is a fresh discovery. But there was very little danger of regarding the preaching of the gospel as dull or too 'traditional', as was sometimes the case later. There was no desire to do and say things differently just for the sake of being different, and hardly any of the negative attitudes to doctrine that developed in some College groups in the late '60s and '70s. Of course the rebels could still go off and join the SCM, and some did so, but to belong to the CICCU was a privilege and a responsibility. It made members realize the necessity of consistency of thought and life, because the rest of the University was watching to see whether a Bible-based Christianity might after all be the answer to the theological wilderness or to the personal sense of emptiness that was fairly common. A small survey done on those who had been CICCU members in one College in 1950 showed that all were active Christians ten years later. There had probably been some 'casualties' among those who professed conversion but never actually joined the CU, but those who got as far as joining had continued consistently.

There was sufficient criticism to keep CICCU members aware that they were a city set on a hill that could not be hid. It was fairly obvious that no other substantial group was offering men and women a salvation that is real. The next fifteen years were not quite so clear cut.

To quote Basil Atkinson again: 'The CICCU was the largest of all University Societies except the Union Society. It had the respect of the University and was recognized as the leading religious society. Thousands of undergraduates heard the gospel during those wonderful years. Hundreds were converted and are in the world somewhere today serving the Master. (The CICCU) was no longer on the defensive. Its message was recognized by many as the genuine truth. There was a positive note of power and of aggressive evangelism.' [66]

Chapter Nine

1955 – 1977
Defence and proclamation

It is not easy to assess correctly events that are very recent in time. For that reason we shall attempt only a brief survey of the last twenty years. It was ushered in, however, by a controversy that highlights some of the important features of the past and of the period under review. This was usually referred to as 'the fundamentalist controversy'.

The fundamentalist controversy

The news that Billy Graham was going to lead the CICCU Mission sparked off a public debate in the correspondence columns of *The Times*. Canon Luce of Durham started it by writing in August 1955, 'The recent increase of fundamentalism among university students cannot but cause concern to those whose work lies in religious education. No branch of education can make terms with an outlook which ignores the conclusions of modern scholarship in that particular department of knowledge. In this connection the proposal that Dr Graham should conduct a mission to Cambridge University raises an issue which does not seem to have been squarely faced by Christians in this country. Universities exist for the advancement of learning; on what basis, therefore, can fundamentalism claim a hearing at Cambridge?' The vicar of Great St Mary's and the Regius Professor of Divinity at Cambridge signed a joint reply to say, in effect, that it wasn't their fault: 'The mission is a private venture, and does not commit the university, or the Church in the university.' Basil Atkinson, in a typically succinct letter, replied 'as one who is proud to be taking a small part in the preparation for Dr Graham's proposed mission'. 'The gospel preached by Dr Graham', he wrote, 'is in accord with true scholarship illuminated by revelation. It originates in the New Testament . . . and it will still be preached when the modernistic concepts of today have been superseded and discarded.' An Assistant Bishop wrote in support of Dr Graham. The Bishop of Durham and several others, some of them the old stalwarts of liberalism, wrote against. G. T. Manley and John Stott and a recent convert from Dr Graham's Harringay crusade joined in. A layman pointedly asked: 'Have your right reverend and reverend correspondents who are opposed to fundamentalism forgotten that at their own ordination they solemnly and publicly declared that they "unfeignedly believed all the canonical scriptures of the Old and New Testament"?'[67]

The controversy continued for some time in other circles. In 1956 two Bishops wrote anti-fundamentalist articles in diocesan papers. The most vigorous, and in many ways the most unexpected, was that of the Bishop of Durham, A. M. Ramsey, who had just been nominated Archbishop of York (later he became Archbishop of Canterbury). In an article on 'The Menace of Fundamentalism' he mentioned Billy Graham and the IVF, offered a caricature of an evangelistic meeting (presumably from second-hand reports), and then wrote, 'He (Billy Graham) has gone. Our English fundamentalism remains. It is *heretical* . . . It is *sectarian* . . . The church must pray that men will be raised up with the power so to preach, that the stream of conversions will not be followed by a backwash of moral casualties and disillusioned sceptics.'[68] What surprised people was that Ramsey was not particularly liberal but was a relatively conservative High-Churchman. His theological lectures in

Cambridge, where he had been a Theology Professor a very short time before, had been appreciated by the CICCU men as some of the most constructive and orthodox of the whole Faculty. The CICCU had even suggested to the Durham University CU that when Ramsey went there as Bishop he might be willing to chair a meeting of the CU Mission. Ramsey knew quite well, however, that the High-Church message was not the same as that of the CICCU. It emerged that he was relatively conservative not so much because of the teaching of the Bible, but rather because of the teaching of the church, that he did not share the CICCU's emphasis on personal faith and new birth and was very unhappy about the emphasis on substitutionary atonement and the final authority and infallibility of the Bible.

It is probably significant that Ramsey had been the student chairman of the introductory meeting of the Willy Nicholson Mission in 1926 (see p. 94 above). Ramsey had then been President of the Union Society. Perhaps he still thought in terms of the reputation of Willy Nicholson. Almost certainly he had been badly briefed by men much more hostile than himself. The fact was that the CICCU men were some of the very few who really believed in the official doctrines of the Church of England as expressed in the Thirty-nine Articles. For Anglicans who were at all liberal to call the CICCU heretical was rather ridiculous. The innuendo of the last sentence about moral casualties seems totally without foundation.

In 1957 the High-Churchman Gabriel Hebert wrote a book which was a more systematic attack. This was entitled *Fundamentalism and the Church of God* (SCM Press, 1957). Hebert attacked conservative evangelicals for their doctrine of Scripture and for their view of the church and its sacraments. This provoked a reply by J. I. Packer in his book *'Fundamentalism' and the Word of God* (IVP, 1958), which has provided the greatest possible help to many generations of students, not least in the CICCU. It is significant that the

High-Church leaders were as worried as the more consistently liberal leaders by the recrudescence of evangelicalism.[69] For the most part they were also mildly liberal in their attitude to the Bible. But they were not rationalists. They believed what they believed because it was the teaching of their church, and a theology that tried to be ruled by evangelical principles – by the death of Christ alone, by faith alone, by the Word of God alone – was no more palatable to most of them than it was to the liberals. Anti-fundamentalism became for a number of years a popular pastime. Rude remarks about Billy Graham or fundamentalists seemed to be a sure way of rousing support for speakers in many different kinds of meetings. Although the High-Church theologians had been drawn in partly because they were more theologically minded than most of the liberals, nevertheless the backbone of the attack was from a more rationalistic standpoint, as Canon Luce's original letter illustrates.

This was by no means the last that was heard of the old-fashioned liberal opposition. It represented the defiant shouts of those who had perhaps begun to realize that the Christian world was turning full circle. Liberalism, which had been launched with such high hopes that it would reach the intelligent unchurched people, had proved a failure in that respect. Meanwhile the supposedly anti-intellectual evangelicals were recapturing the minds of intelligent and educated young people as well as the uneducated. This was happening in a way that confounded their critics. The protest was the despairing cry of men who could do nothing to stop the tide but who sincerely believed it to be a major disaster. High-Church leaders such as Ramsey and Hebert also saw their own party in the church beginning to decline and the evangelicals gaining an increasing percentage of ordinands for the Church of England. As the Bishop of Southwell (F. R. Barry) said in a speech in the Convocation of York, 'It was a pretty serious business for the Church of

England if any very considerable or increasing proportion of its ministry was going to be recruited with an outlook and an approach of that kind.'[70] There were similarities to the feelings of the conservative evangelicals in the parishes when liberalism seemed to be carrying all before it in the Universities in the 1900–1925 period. In this case, however, the old guard (liberal and High-Church) was overwhelmingly strong in the teaching and preaching posts in the Universities. Nevertheless they still could not persuade the students that they had the answer. The 1955 generation of evangelicals largely ignored what the liberals were saying and set about trying to rebuild student witness (and, when they went down from University, church life) on biblical foundations. A few of the more scholarly men among them read the current theology carefully, obtained first-class degrees and post-graduate qualifications, and tried to start rebuilding an evangelical theology.

A new situation

In many ways the Stott Mission of 1952 was the climax, but the Billy Graham Mission of 1955 and the second Stott Mission in 1958 carried on the work. Both created opposition, as was inevitable. Stott gave less offence because he was harder to dismiss in the University. No-one could deny his right to be heard and what he said had to be reckoned with as an exposition of New Testament Christianity. Graham could be more easily dismissed as 'an American Revivalist' and his stronger pressure for decision was an obvious target of criticism by some.

There was now (in the late fifties) a new situation. For decades the other religious groups had regarded the CICCU as an almost negligible side-show in the religious scene. They now woke up to the fact that it was the largest and most lively force at the undergraduate level. It could not be ignored. If its members did not attend Chapel (they usually did in fair numbers), the Chapel would as a rule be relatively empty. However far removed they were theologically, a growing number of Chaplains began to be more friendly in their attitude towards the CICCU.

By 1955 the SCM was declining and even the denominational societies, which had had a short revival, had reached, and in some cases already passed, a peak from which they mostly steadily fell away.[71] The ex-war-service generation was finishing. The new students were younger and less religious. Humanism began to gain ground. For an increasing number of students it was a choice between no religion at all or an out-and-out religion which was not afraid to be definite about the faith. Some CICCU College freshers' squashes changed from a bland theme such as 'Christianity in University Life', which had been the familiar title, to themes such as 'God has spoken'. Freshers' evangelism was very important. Every College had a meeting at which the elements of the gospel were explained. Many whose interest was aroused then went on to become Christians at the freshers' sermon or later in the first term. Most of those converted in this period were probably first-year students.

The CICCU brought up a very strong team of speakers for these freshers' squashes each year and made this outreach a major effort. But gradually the emphasis on the freshers' squashes as an initial evangelistic outreach declined. By 1965 most Colleges had lapsed into a meeting at which CU members talked harmlessly about the activities of the CICCU – until some older members urged that the opportunity be not missed. The defence was that they wanted to show that the CICCU was human – something that was hardly in doubt. Nevertheless it could be true that the freshers' squashes had sometimes been too aggressive. But this change also represented a weakening of the ideal of the CICCU as essentially a witness – an evangelistic body rather than just a fellowship. It was not until 1970 that the situation was restored.

The 1960s

The CICCU has not always gone on from strength to strength. It is difficult to be certain why the 1960s was a rather disappointing period. Perhaps we are too near in time to judge. A good solid work was done. The evangelistic ideal was by no means lost, and compared with most other bodies it was very fruitful. It became accepted that at least a third of the members (it had probably been over a half in the 1950s) had become personal Christians since coming up. When one could have hoped for striking advances, however, they did not come until a new surge of life made itself felt in 1969–71.

There is no doubt that the University became more hostile to Christian influences in the 1960s. In 1960 the College Chapels were well attended; by 1967 they were relatively empty. The DPM correspondingly declined from forty or fifty in 1960, with a hundred plus on Sundays, to a very low ebb by 1967. Sometimes the numbers were only in single figures. The CICCU Sunday night evangelistic sermon audiences also declined. There was talk of discontinuing both DPM and the sermons. There was uncertainty among the leaders. The new generation of students seemed to be more careless and more conceited. It was not so easy to get a good audience and the CICCU members had to work harder to bring their friends. The Mission in 1961 (led by Kenneth Prior) was hard going and numbers built up only slowly. But God blessed once more and there are quite a few now active in Christian life and witness who became Christians during this time. When attendance at DPM was made a major topic for prayer it gradually recovered.

The CICCU also faced some new internal problems. Around 1960 a very strongly Calvinistic group emerged. At first it led to a sharp polarization: people were either ardently for it or strongly against it. Because its criticism of CICCU traditions concentrated on the methods and

142

content of evangelism, it left some members too uncertain of themselves to get on with the job. It was argued, for instance, that Revelation 3:20, which had been a favourite evangelistic verse for many, should not be used in evangelism. Even John 3:16 came under fire as a text for this purpose. At first the CICCU Exec. over-reacted a little but then, partly with the sane advice of Basil Atkinson and others, allowed the conflict to blow itself out. The more Calvinistic brought with them a very helpful emphasis on biblical doctrine and on the value of some of the older Puritans and similar more modern literature. When the polarization died down all were able to work together again with mutual benefit.

As has frequently happened elsewhere, the strong Calvinistic influence was followed by a swing to a charismatic influence. At first the CICCU leadership reacted even more strongly to this, especially as it derived from independent visiting speakers who set up their own groups in some Colleges. The charismatics tended to regard the doctrinal emphasis of the more Calvinistic and the debates it had engendered as very unprofitable. The CICCU leaders feared that the charismatic groups would lead to so much concentration on fellowship and self-improvement that the evangelistic thrust would be lost. They had feared the same result from the Calvinistic influence. Both these emphases were really new in the CICCU. It had been mildly 'Reformed' all along, with its emphasis on grace, and it had stressed the work of the Holy Spirit along Keswick lines. But it had not included any appreciable number of strong representatives of either emphasis before.[72]

Whatever the reasons, the sixties did see the CICCU rather more taken up with its own internal problems. It became all too easy for a Christian fresher to be so smothered with Christian friendship that when he had found his feet at the end of the first term he had very few non-Christian friends. The responsibility to be a soul-winner was not so obviously laid on all the members. This had the advantage that the less extrovert people felt more at home in the CU, but it also meant that there was a certain loss of vision for the CICCU as above all an agency for witness to non-Christians.

Arts Faculty witness

There followed another change which was entirely for the good. During the Second World War the CICCU had overwhelmingly consisted of scientists, engineers and medicals; no-one else much was able to stay for more than six or twelve months, because of the call-up. This emphasis continued to a considerable extent after the war. In the sixties there came into the CU a growing proportion of students in the Arts Faculties and this was not at first so easy to cope with. These members wanted to develop activities for arts students and there was relatively little senior help or even good literature to guide them. Between the wars the bigger apologetic debates had seemed to be on the science and religion question and some evangelical literature on these aspects had been published. By the sixties there was an excellent group of professors of science and medicine available to speak. There was hardly a single evangelical professor (and very few lecturers) in the fields of history, literature, languages, economics, politics or philosophy. Evangelical students in these fields began to discover that the apologetic questions were as important here as anywhere else, and the CICCU began to branch out in its concerns. A successful visit by Professor Rookmaaker (Professor of the History of Art at the Free University, Amsterdam) was arranged by the Exec. in 1969 and surprised some people by the number of students it attracted and interested. By the 1970s there were excellent groups working in several of these fields. Some groups produced plays and other activities to try to reach their section of the University better. There was healthy debate about the scope of such things, but no-one was now criticized for having an interest in contemporary culture.

Apologetics

The 1971 Mission (led by Michael Green) included pre-Mission activities on a new scale, to reach every section of the University. Eighty musicians, for instance, came to a special meeting for that department. The magazine *Really*, which started in 1968 and became established about 1970, was an unofficial effort to reach out and was often very competent. By this time it was a matter of course for CICCU members to be interested in the application of biblical truth to their academic field, whatever it was, whereas such a concern had been unusual in the forties and even rather suspect in the twenties.

Over the same period there began to be a change in the style of some of the central evangelistic activities. In the late 1950s a series of apologetic addresses was launched, again on mid-week evenings. This time they were much more successful and were very well attended. They did not altogether please those who felt that the CU should keep to 'the simple gospel'. Significantly there were very few old CICCU men available as speakers. Most of those who came to speak were from other less ivory-tower Universities where the Christians, as students or research students, had been pushed more vigorously into debate. Almost immediately it became clear that these lectures would reach some who did not go to church and did not come to CICCU sermons. The knowledge that one or two had gone on to attend CICCU sermons and been converted was a great encouragement. By 1970 an experiment was carried out in holding two lectures a term on a Sunday night in the Senate House instead of the sermon which had been held weekly, usually in Holy Trinity Church, since the 1920s. The aim was to reach the less religious who would not easily come into a church and for whom Sunday night was nevertheless far more likely to be free than a week-night. These lectures have continued irregularly and undoubtedly have reached new people, often drawing in far more students than the sermons, though inevitably giving a less solid biblical content because the speakers had to keep to their subjects. Probably no-one thinks of this as a substitute for preaching, but it was a preparation, and there were conversions in personal talks after these lectures. Nevertheless the Sunday night (8.30 p.m.) sermons (now called 'addresses') remained a main means of evangelism and every member was encouraged to bring a friend. From this point on, however, they were not held every week. The occasional Sunday was left free for the lectures or for College-based evangelism arranged by each College group independently.

Meanwhile the theological pressures seemed as strong as, if less extreme than, before. A very large number of CICCU members read theology, sometimes constituting a high proportion of the Faculty. By no means all could stand up to the constant pressure to move away from a conservative evangelical position and there was still a steady trickle of men lost to the CICCU because their studies drew them to another outlook. This problem was nothing like as serious as it had been in the thirties, partly because there was more help. The Theological Students' Fellowship of the IVF, for instance, promoted literature, conferences and speakers. It was also partly because the members had not started from such an extreme black-and-white position themselves and therefore could appreciate some good in the course without feeling threatened.

A weak period

To go back a little, the period 1965–69 was really a relatively low point in the post-Second World War period. Outwardly the CICCU had strong numbers and it was still doing very good work, but it had lost some of its vigour. It is true that the sheer size of the CU – now about 400 – forced the

College groups to take the main load of fellowship and evangelism. Some Colleges had their own DPM. The Exec. were torn between the desire to encourage groups at the College level and the desire to maintain a stronger central fellowship and witness. There was a short period when a good many (including some of the Exec.) were all for reducing central activities to a minimum.

In 1968 a group of College reps wrote to all the members criticizing the central programme, including DPM. That was the turning-point and members began once more to see that such united activities were very important. DPM numbers increased again and support for sermons improved when the alternatives were really faced. In fact the DPM increased from the day that people met to pray about the possibility of discontinuing it! In January 1970 an excellent preterminal house-party with a great spirit of prayer marked the change. The General Committee (*i.e.* College reps) voted overwhelmingly to continue the DPM.[73]

From this discussion the CU emerged with an emphasis on the College group as a means of fellowship and Bible study, but with renewed emphasis on the DPM and on other central activities for teaching (Saturday Bible readings) and evangelism (the Sunday sermons and lectures).

The 1970s

During the 1970s the CICCU has grown very considerably. Undoubtedly students have become more interested in religion. As one Christian fresher remarked, 'Almost everyone is willing to talk seriously about Christian things if given the opportunity.' A large 'fringe' of the kind of people who, in the 1930s, would have been out of earshot of the CICCU and busy in SCM or the Chapel, were now fairly frequent attenders, though not usually members. Such a 'fringe' offered enormous possibilities and certainly represented an opportunity on a new scale. Many of those who now came to the CICCU had never been evangelicals and only gradually or partially came to an evangelical standpoint as they studied the Bible or listened to Bible readings and sermons. The result was that the CICCU was a little less clearly defined and there were rather more people within its circle who grumbled about the strong and consistently evangelical programme.

The freshers' programme had revived by 1970 and, apart from the primary function of reaching freshers, it often served to unite the College groups, which were now increasingly called 'College CUs'. As one rep. in a somewhat divided College wrote: 'To have a definite aim (the freshers' work) really caused the group to come together in fellowship in a natural way (rather than introspective). Prayer meetings were full of prayer and expectancy! Instead of "we are going to enjoy warm fellowship", suddenly we had common prayer needs and concerns, which welded the group together.' The freshers' outreach was something that all the second- and third-year members did together and it set a pattern for the year. In this period, also, many College CUs started holding their own house-parties – perhaps with one or two other Colleges. But after the 1960s' period of uncertainty, the DPM, sermons, missions and Saturday night Bible readings were strengthened again. Missionary activities were also continued on a united basis and the College reps realized afresh the value of the wider fellowship of the CICCU and their official links with an Exec. member. There was renewed growth and in this the Missions of 1971 and 1974 played a substantial part. Both were marked by good attendances (up to 1,000 each night) and large numbers professing conversion. There was an increasing flow of Christian freshers, with a considerable sprinkling of those who had been abroad in missionary situations or similar service overseas between leaving school and going up to University. They came up with rather more experience and maturity than the average Christian student and played an active and effective part in personal evangelism from the very start. The number of those professing conversion increased again, so that half the members were fairly new Christians.

By 1977 the CICCU finds itself strong numerically. The formal membership may be less than 450, but perhaps twice that number or more are in Bible study groups every week. The DPM is not large on most days, but can reach 100 on Saturdays to pray for the week-end. In many Colleges the prayer life is strong. Evangelistic Bible studies – special groups consisting usually of two Christians and four to six non-Christians meeting for weekly study – have been a feature in addition to the usual College group Bible studies. These represent a sign of the times in that to so many freshers the Bible is almost unknown and therefore interesting. These have proved a major means of evangelism and it has been found that many of those professing conversion have been attending them or the regular Bible studies for some time. More of those professing conversion are second- or third-year students, perhaps because, being almost without Christian background, they need longer to understand the message. Some College groups now have up to seventy members. This is too large to meet together in College rooms and therefore they are divided up into numerous Bible study groups. In many Colleges the CICCU members between them know almost everyone in the College. In a survey in 1976, before the Mission of 1977, it was not difficult to allocate responsibility for inviting every student since, even in the largest College, nearly every student was known by a CU member personally. Whether they also understood the gospel is another question – hence the Mission and its attempt to reach out to the whole university. But the 'coverage' was there if members were able to use the opportunities effectively. One constantly heard from those who professed conversion that their interest and concern were aroused by what they saw in the lives of their Christian friends. Clearly the effective witness of the CU could be very much larger if there is this enormous range of personal contacts.

Cambridge is no longer so important in the national life as it once was. There are now many other excellent universities and in any case a degree is no longer such a necessary stepping-stone to leadership. Nevertheless there must be few churches or other local Christian groups that draw in 300 or so young people every year and each year send out an equal number to scatter all over the world. Having said that, however, the CICCU needs to ask why it should not be 600 each year in the very favoured circumstances of their residential community.

If the CICCU can maintain its clear witness to biblical truth while it continues to expand its outreach, the possibilities are thrilling. In order to keep true it may from time to time have to lose members, who are no longer in sympathy, as it did in 1910, the 1920s and the 1930s particularly. For many years CICCU leaders used to pray that they would gain the position of being the main representatives of Christianity in the University. They were anxious that, if people became spiritually hungry, they would turn where a straightforward biblical message would be heard. Now that that prayer has been largely answered at the undergraduate level, it is a tremendous responsibility before God to make the gospel known clearly and widely – if possible throughout the University and then carry it all over the world.

Retrospect and prospect

In many ways the 1977 position is similar to that of the 1890s. The CICCU is known by almost every undergraduate. It has the ear of many who are not personal Christians and God is doing a great and lasting work in many lives. The comparison with 1890, however, poses two questions. First, how far is there a danger of making the same mistakes as in the 1890s? If the CICCU has grown prosperous, it will obviously face the temptation to be careless about its doctrinal stand, the identity of its witness and its aims. Just when all seemed to be so successful in that earlier period, the gospel that was preached began to be undermined in a way that finally left only a remnant to carry on the work. It is vital that we learn from that history. Secondly, we must ask whether today we have anything like the evangelistic zeal of our predecessors. Occasionally today we hear again the note of 'the evangelization of the world in this generation'. But are we back in the situation where a College group will make sure that every fresher has a chance to talk over the claims of Christ? If zeal for dangerous missionary service in remote places is qualified by concern for darker parts of Britain also, does the CICCU see itself as a task force set for the evangelization of Cambridge, then of Britain, and then of the uttermost parts of the earth? There was something genuinely New Testament about the evangelistic zeal of those in that earlier generation. Have we recaptured it, even if the form of its expression is different?

Finally we may ask another question. What factors, if we can identify them, have constituted the golden thread providing continuity and consistency in the CICCU? To that the author may perhaps be allowed to offer some sort of answer. The only thread which has at all times and places kept the CICCU both alive and true to the gospel has been the constant exposure to the Bible. The Quiet Time, College Bible readings, and the Saturday and Sunday meetings have by and large exposed the CICCU members to a barrage of life-giving biblical teaching and application. That has both challenged and created life and has kept the personal and corporate life purged and the evangelism not too far from the New Testament model. It is not of course the bare ideas of the Bible. As this history has illustrated, it has often needed a special touch of the fresh experience of the Holy Spirit to bring orthodox religion to reality and life. God has been pleased by His Spirit to make the Bible the life-giving stream and guide. There has been a repeated fresh discovery of biblical truth and life rather than a mere maintenance of an orthodox system of doctrine. And yet the basic doctrine has been clear, and has been kept clear with considerable difficulty and contention. It has been the essential backbone. The CICCU leaders have been prepared to define the gospel which is the power of God, even when the learned world found it least acceptable. Whatever other people thought, the CICCU has sought to be loyal to God's living Word. Loyalty is not a popular idea. But the CICCU believed that, since God has spoken, our part is to obey what He requires and to tell out what He declares. Sometimes these things are hidden from the wise and prudent and revealed unto babes. If God has spoken, who are we to hesitate?

For many years the CICCU Missionary Prayer Card bore as a motto the words of Revelation 12:11, 'They overcame him by the blood of the Lamb, and by the word of their testimony; and they loved not their lives unto the death.' May that always be true.

Perhaps the most fitting perspective on these hundred years is in the words of Psalm 103:15–16 and 1 Peter 1:24, 25.

'As for man, his days are like grass;
   he flourishes like a flower of the field;
for the wind passes over it, and it is gone,
   and its place knows it no more.
But the steadfast love of the Lord is from everlasting to
      everlasting upon those who fear him,
   and his righteousness to children's children,
to those who keep his covenant
   and remember to do his commandments.'

'For
   "All flesh is like grass
      and all its glory like the flower of grass.
      The grass withers, and the flower falls,
      but the word of the Lord abides for ever."
That word is the good news which was preached to you.'

Notes

Chapter 1

1 The Cambridge University Act of 1856 (effective 1858) allowed students to enrol, hold scholarships and take BA degrees without religious tests. It was still necessary, however, to agree to the Thirty-nine Articles of the Church of England in order to be an MA or hold any office. All University teachers were therefore still Church of England. In 1871, by the University Tests Act, religious tests were removed from all lay offices (the Divinity Faculty staff, therefore, remained Anglican). King's College, London and Durham University were also strongly Anglican and the latter was not freed from tests until this 1871 Act. University College, London was a 'secular' foundation supported by many Nonconformists as well as Jeremy Bentham and his friends. To put this in its more human context, the author's paternal grandfather had to go to University College, London, rather than to Oxford or Cambridge, where friends and relatives were, because he was a Quaker and as a matter of principle did not feel free to sign the Articles.

2 We shall use the word 'evangelical' in this book in the sense in which it is generally used in Britain (see J. R. W. Stott, *Christ the Controversialist* (IVP, 1970), Introductory Essay B). In other countries it sometimes carries a different sense, but here it means that section of the Christian community that emphasizes the reliability and final authority of the Bible (over reason, tradition, the Pope, *etc.*) and whose message focuses on the finished work of Christ on the cross for our forgiveness, so that we cannot add to what He has done by works, rituals or spiritual earnestness. It can be characterized in the phrase 'by Christ alone, through faith alone, from Scripture alone'.

3 The University at this time was sharply divided between the 'undergraduates' and the 'senior members of the University'. There were few who came in between. We shall, in this book, refer to the latter as 'the seniors'. At this stage they were mostly members of teaching staff who held a life 'Fellowship' in one of the Colleges and dined at a College High Table. The teaching staff were popularly called 'dons' and, since dons were all single and lived in College, the word 'donnish' has become a synonym for academic eccentricity. The nearest equivalent in modern

speech, perhaps, is 'the absent-minded professor'. Today College Fellowships are no longer held for life and most Fellows are married and live out of College. There is also now a large group of research students and other graduate students who dine with the undergraduates. This is chiefly, however, a post-1939 development. In Simeon's time and nearly up to the Second World War, there was a big gap between the undergraduates and the senior members of the University. The latter expected to be treated with considerable respect as the leaders of the University and thought of themselves as forming the minds of the young.

4 Simeon started with William Law's *The Whole Duty of Man*. This was the only religious book he knew of and it started the process in his mind. Bishop Thomas Wilson's *A Short and Plain Instruction for the Lord's Supper* (1733) brought him to assurance of salvation through faith in the substitutionary death of Christ.

5 A student who had come to scoff was heard to say, on leaving the church, ' "Well, Simeon is no fool however!" "Fool!" replied his companion, "did you ever hear such a sermon before?" ' (H. C. G. Moule, *Charles Simeon* (1892; reissued IVP, 1948), p. 64).

6 They were pupils at the school called Liverpool College. Both had been influenced by the widespread religious revival of 1859, which had deeply affected the churches in America and all over Britain.

7 Girton College for women was started in 1869 with five students at Hitchin, twenty-seven miles away. In 1873 it was moved to Girton Village, very properly nearly two miles outside Cambridge! Newnham College started in Cambridge in 1871, also with five students. In 1873 the first three women (from Girton) took the Degree examination and passed. But women were not fully members of the University until 1948. Up to that point one had to refer to 'members of the University and of the Women's Colleges' if one wished to include both men and women. University education for women was regarded as very *avant garde* at this time.

8 The Brethren movement began in Dublin in the late 1820s and spread quickly to England. In its early days it drew a great deal of its support from the upper middle class and in this respect differed from some other forms of nineteenth-century nonconformity. By the time the CICCU was founded a definite

Brethren association had been built up in a number of such families. Since it was customary for children from these homes to go to University, Brethren ideas soon made themselves felt in the CICCU in spite of the very strong Anglican influence in the University. There were soon also a number of Quakers in the CICCU for similar reasons. The President in 1900, for instance, was a Quaker and several others were from Quaker stock, though now members of the Church of England.

9 See J. C. Pollock, *The Cambridge Seven* (IVP, 1955), p. 26. Waldegrave was the son of the evangelical peer, Lord Radstock, who, while he himself never broke his links with the Church of England, was an accepted speaker and leader among the Brethren. Robert Armitage's comment was a verbal one made to the author in about 1950. Armitage became MP for Leeds.

10 S. A. Blackwood, a civil servant, later Sir Arthur Blackwood, head of the Post Office.

11 This was a conference by invitation of William Cowper-Temple, MP (author of the influential Cowper-Temple Clause on Religious Education) at his large country house at Broadlands, Hampshire.

12 Even in 1898 there were only three officers who formed a sort of unofficial executive committee. The rest of the business was settled by the meeting of College reps. This seems to have been very infrequent. They all met individually of course from time to time at the DPM. It was not until 1910 that a more formal executive committee was elected by the College reps' meeting which became the General Committee.

13 The Cambridge Colleges were then fairly small communities, most of them of only about one hundred students. Nearly everyone lived in College. There were a few non-collegiate students who could not afford College fees (these formed Fitzwilliam House later and that is now a full College of the University). In 1977 there are twenty-five Colleges, the largest being Trinity College with 750 undergraduates and over 200 graduate students. In the 1870s many Colleges had a distinctive character; King's, for instance, contained largely Old Etonians. Trinity (not to be confused with another smaller College, Trinity Hall, nor with Holy Trinity Church) had a good many aristocrats and was also the centre of advance in physics. Caius had a reputation for medicine. It was therefore a significant step to get every College of the University represented.

Chapter 2

14 G. M. Davies, *A Chaplain in India* (Marshall, Morgan and Scott, 1933). Davies went to Cambridge in 1878 as a non-collegiate student for the first year, because his father was an impecunious parson. His total expenses for fees and board and lodging for that year were £63 1s. 7d.

15 Up to the 1940s undergraduates and BAs had to wear an academic gown and mortarboard ('cap and gown') outside College after dark. They could thereby be distinguished, at a glance, by towns-people and senior members of the University. Failure to keep this rule resulted in a fine of 6s. 8d. (*i.e.* one-third of a pound) if you were met by a Proctor and your name and address taken. Proctors were, and are, the disciplinary officers of the University.

16 Buxton was brought along by his father. He was at the time a recent graduate but, like many others, especially prominent sportsmen (he had played tennis for the University), he had kept up some links with University life. He came from a truly Christian background but was not, up to this point, personally trusting Christ. This was typical of many sons of evangelical families who were helped in the Mission. Buxton later became a leading missionary in Japan.

17 The Backs are the large area of grass and trees behind the Colleges and bordering the river Cam.

18 Quoted in E. S. Woods and F. B. MacNutt, *Theodore, Bishop of Winchester* (SPCK, 1933). The references to 'Woods' are to Theodore Woods (see pp. 33, 88, 89).

19 E. S. Woods and F. B. MacNutt, *op. cit.*, p. 16.

20 Moule was Norissian Professor of Divinity at Cambridge before he went to be Principal of Ridley Hall. This move (really a step down academically) represented his concern with, and gifts for, pastoral rather than merely academic theology, and from then on he ceased to do much battle in the increasingly critical and arid theological world, though he wrote excellent commentaries.

Chapter 3

21 See J. C. Pollock, *The Cambridge Seven* (IVP, 1955) and N. P. Grubb, *C. T. Studd: Cricketer and Pioneer* (Lutterworth Press, 1933).

22 Eugene Stock, *The History of the Church Missionary Society* (CMS, 1899), Vol. II, pp. 46f. and Vol. III, pp. 33f. and 354. The CIM records do not tell us which of their missionaries had been at Cambridge.

23 The earliest basis (1886) was, 'We are willing and desirous, God permitting, to become foreign missionaries.' At Moody's Mount Hermon conference in 1886, where Wilder and his sister had prayed for one hundred volunteers, exactly one hundred signed that declaration. See R. P. Wilder, *The Student Volunteer Movement* (SVM, New York, 1938). The American movement was called 'The Student Volunteer Movement for Foreign Missions' and the British 'The Student Volunteer Missionary Union'.

24 R. P. Wilder, *The Great Commission* (Oliphants, 1936), p. 46. Cambridge of course had already sent notable missionaries abroad, of whom Henry Martyn was the most famous.

25 Much of this chapter is culled from Tissington Tatlow's official account, *The Story of the Student Christian Movement of Great Britain and Ireland* (SCM, 1933), especially chapters 2, 3 and 4. See in particular pp. 48–62 and see chapter 5 for the Liverpool Conference. See also R. P. Wilder's books.

26 Basil Matthews in his biography, *John R. Mott, World Citizen* (SCM, 1934), p. 165, quotes a Cambridge student describing his 1908 visit: 'The meeting on the fourth night (of a six-day mission) defies description. It seems to belong to the land of dreams and impossibilities . . . 1,250 present . . . An after meeting was held at which 560 remained; never before have we seen University men jumping over forms to secure good seats at an after meeting.'

27 The 1897 diary of the CICCU President (D. B. Barclay) describes his life both before and after he took office. His day included an average of six hours' work six days a week. This was meticulously recorded so as to ensure that he reached the target. He usually worked all morning and then attended DPM before lunch. There was occasional squash or tennis in the afternoon and an hour or two walking or cycling with friends (often tandem and once a trip up the St Neots Road on a friend's motor tricycle!). There was constant entertaining of a group of a dozen or so friends, and frequent callers and calls on people concerned with the CICCU, including G. T. Manley, then a Fellow, and the two ordained members of the Cambridge Pastorate (Dodderidge and Armitage). It was usual to have friends to breakfast, lunch and

tea, or to go out for these meals. Sunday included College Chapel (attendance was compulsory twice during the week as well as on Sunday), a prayer meeting for old boys of his school, sometimes a College Bible study run by senior men, the CICCU sermon (150–300 present) followed by a squash with the same speaker (usually twenty-five or so present), or in the summer an Open-air on Parker's Piece instead of both. This, however, left time for reading and a walk! He did not teach in a Sunday School, perhaps because he had been Secretary of the CMU and responsible for the CICCU/OICCU Conference before he joined the Executive Committee. He often attended CMU meetings. There was no CICCU activity at the College level, so that the DPM and Sunday activities were the main things apart from vacation conferences and the warm and stimulating friendships which included informal prayer and sometimes Bible study as a normal close to their tea-parties and evening discussions.

28 Tissington Tatlow, *op. cit.*, p. 33.

29 *E.g.* Professor E. T. Whittaker, quoted in E. S. Woods and F. B. MacNutt, *Theodore, Bishop of Winchester*, pp. 16 and 25. See also their comments about Theodore Woods.

Chapter 4

30 Tissington Tatlow, *The Story of the Student Christian Movement*, pp. 220 and 272.

31 See, for example, pp. 36f. of the third edition (1891): 'It is inconceivable that the Israelites should have brought with them out of the desert a cultus they observed in the time of the kings (Exodus 22, 23 and 24), which throughout presupposed the fields and gardens of Palestine; they borrowed it from the Canaanites.' See also pp. 21, 53, *etc.* That could be called unscholarly speculation dressed up in a dogmatic assertion. At the time it was thought to be very scientific and scholarly by all but a few. Basically it was not 'rational' – it did not follow reasonably and necessarily from the actual data. It imposed upon the Bible its own criteria of what seemed reasonable to the modern man and ignored those data that did not fit in. As time went on that left less and less of biblical truth still to be believed. This *rationalistic* approach makes 'what seems reasonable to me and my circle' the final test of what shall be accepted. Reason is made into a bed of Procrustes (Procrustes

was that unsavoury character of Greek mythology whose guests were either stretched out to the full length of his bed or else cut down so that they fitted it exactly). A *rational* approach may mean, however, the very opposite of that – a sitting under the facts to make sure that our reasoning follows faithfully from whatever data we have been given. In this sense science is rational but not rationalistic. The approach of Wellhausen and the Higher Critics generally was rationalistic and therefore to modern eyes seems unscientific and unscholarly in the strict sense of those terms. It was, however, immensely attractive because it fitted the Bible into the popular philosophical framework by cutting out the points that did not match and finding plausible reasons for doing so, as in the quotation above. It was believed that it would make it easier for people to accept the message of the Bible.

Many evangelicals (and others) over-reacted and became hostile to any use of reason or scholarly study of the Bible. They forgot that while reason is fallen, so are all our other faculties, and that if reasoning is kept in its proper place as a humble tool of understanding God-given data, it is a part of being a human being to use, rather than purely emotional or imaginative approaches to understand the Bible under the guidance of the Holy Spirit. Lower Criticism (which includes much scholarly textual criticism) must not be confused with Higher Criticism. By Lower Criticism is usually meant the attempt to discover the best text and its exact meaning without any 'Higher' principle to control the results.

32 Canon Charles Smyth in a lecture at Cambridge. He also stressed the damage to the spirit of evangelicals from the lawsuits in which they became involved when they tried to exclude ritualistic practices. The second point, however, hardly applied to Cambridge.

33 See Tissington Tatlow, *op. cit.*

34 SCM archives, Birmingham: letter dated 8 October 1910 to Miss E. A. Constable, a student at the Royal Free Hospital who wrote objecting to what Peake had said at the conference.

35 By 1918 the CMS Committee was also sharply divided and in 1922 even the CMS itself (although broadly evangelical) lost a substantial group of missionaries and supporters to form the new Bible Churchmen's Missionary Society. It is interesting that several of the older CICCU stalwarts, including G. T. Manley, did not join the BCMS, although they were upset by what was happening in the CMS. They believed that there was need for a

far tougher policy in the student world than they felt was essential in some church contexts.

36 John R. Mott was very emphatic about leaving Keswick. See SCM archives.

37 SCM archives: letter from F. H. Mosse, dated 28 January 1912.

38 Mother SCM, however, was also becoming more interested in social application of Christianity than in missionary study or evangelistic work. We shall discuss this question in chapter 6. Some, like Wilder, believed that this was a cause of decline; others believed it was rather a result of losing the biblical priorities. In any case students in the SCM were being led by their senior friends into increasingly sophisticated social studies and the CICCU held back.

39 The Mission is described in note 26, above.

40 Morris became a missionary Bishop of North Africa. Mowll became, first, a Bishop in China and then Archbishop of Sydney. Mowll was President of the CICCU for five terms and exerted a strong influence until ordination in 1913. His ordination, however, was blocked by the Bishop of Ely who refused to license him when he was invited to be curate of Holy Trinity Church, Cambridge. This was almost certainly because of his uncompromising stand, as there was no other apparent reason. He then went to Wycliffe College, Toronto, and later to China. See Marcus Loane's biography, which has a full account of the whole Cambridge period from Mowll's point of view.

Chapter 5

41 Verbal communication with R. L. Pelly before he died in 1976 confirms this. Ben Harder obtained an interview (see Acknowledgments).

42 If this sounds conceited about the influence of Cambridge, it must be remembered that it was, for a long time, a cause of complaint by others that nearly all the influential posts in the Church of England were held by Oxford or Cambridge men. They were influential out of all proportion to their numbers and they also still provided, between them, a large majority of the ordinands for the Church of England ministry. Oxford and Cambridge graduates also provided important lay leadership in many of the

professions. It was only after the Second World War that this situation was totally changed.

43 For instance, the evangelical societies working in South America were excluded from the 1910 Edinburgh Missionary Conference as a condition laid down by certain High-Church leaders for their attendance at it. See also note 40, above.

44 See Tissington Tatlow, *The Story of the Student Christian Movement*, p. 486. The new Basis read: 'In joining this union I declare my faith in God through Jesus Christ, whom as Saviour and Lord I desire to serve.' Of the delegates at the SCM General Committee 364 voted in favour and twenty-eight against.

45 Although they were not using it, the SCM wished to retain the title LICCU for London when evangelical groups were re-formed there. So the title London Inter-Faculty Christian Union (LIFCU) was used instead.

46 This was published by Marshall, Morgan and Scott and was only thirty-five pages long. The text was signed (initials only) by six CICCU leaders including the first three Presidents since disaffiliation. Handley Moule, who was by then Bishop of Durham, wrote a foreword.

47 Howard Mowll made this comment from personal knowledge of the men. See Marcus Loane's biography.

48 Some who would not speak of Christ's deity spoke of His 'divinity', but meant far less than that He was God. At the conference in 1906 some students had been shocked by a speaker who would go no further than to say that Jesus 'has to us the value of Deity' (verbal communication from Mrs G. R. Barclay, née Watney).

49 Oliver Tomkins, *The Life of Edward Woods* (SCM, 1957), p. 56.

50 *Ibid.*, p. 56. Edward Woods wrote in 1921, 'Whatever else is obscure to me, this then I am beginning at least to see with absolute clearness, and that is that Christianity is really intended to provide a glowing comprehensive fellowship for all who can call Jesus Lord and slave for His Kingdom.'

51 Memorandum by Norman P. Grubb.

Chapter 6

52 E. S. Woods and F. B. MacNutt, *Theodore, Bishop of Winchester*, p. 132.

53 The Union Society in Cambridge was the Debating Society and club, with restaurant and library, and was not automatically joined by students as in most other Universities. The President in 1926 was A. M. Ramsey (later Archbishop of Canterbury).

54 C. E. Raven, *The Wanderers' Way* (1928). In spite of his aggressive liberalism Raven had extraordinary charm and influence. There are many stories about him. For instance, when invited at a ceremony in Ely Cathedral to 'Stand over there, Raven; you will make a fine splash of red' (*i.e.* in his Doctor of Divinity's gown), he replied, 'I was not ordained to be a splash of red!'

55 H. Earnshaw Smith (1923–26, part-time), Hugh R. Gough (1927), Norman Grubb (1929) and Kenneth Hooker (1929–30).

56 *A Brief History of the Inter-Varsity Fellowship of Evangelical Christian Unions* (IVFECU, no date, but evidently late 1928), pp. 27, 9, 19.

57 The Inter-Varsity Conference was held annually from 1919 onwards and each year appointed a committee to plan the next one and a secretary who, from 1924 onwards, was Douglas Johnson. In 1928 this Conference created the Inter-Varsity Fellowship of Evangelical Christian Unions, with thirteen Universities affiliated, in Aberdeen, Belfast, Bristol, Cambridge (men's and women's CUs), Cardiff, Dublin (men's and women's CUs), Edinburgh, Glasgow, Liverpool, London, Manchester, Oxford and St Andrews. See *A Brief History of the IVFECU*. Douglas Johnson was Secretary of the IVF until 1964. He always denied that he had any serious influence, but all those who benefited from his friendship knew otherwise.

58 Cambridge University Missionary Band letter, 28 August 1922.

Chapter 7

59 His mother and then his sister also helped to provide admirable Sunday teas and other hospitality at their house in Grange Road. There are many humorous 'Basil At.' stories still in circulation; but the fact that he was the subject of so many jokes made his overwhelmingly strong views bearable and wholesome.

60 This was the author, and he did not take the advice given to him !

61 This was Derek Kidner (later Warden of Tyndale House). He had
   studied music in London and was a skilled performer. He now
   came up to Cambridge to read theology. The CICCU were
   delighted when their President was the performer at a public
   concert in the Guildhall and even more delighted when he got a
   first-class degree in theology. He represented and, to his own
   generation, set the example of a more positive attitude to
   theology. John Wenham, who had graduated in 1935, was a
   fairly frequent visitor trying to stir up the TSF and to help
   individuals. Each generation needed fresh leaders in this relatively
   new trend and John Wenham tried to spot the men who could do
   it and to encourage them both in Cambridge and elsewhere. He
   constantly lent and gave important books to students, to their
   great benefit.

62 Sir Frederick Catherwood had no active interest in such subjects
   while he was an undergraduate, but when, later, he got together
   a group of evangelicals to write papers which eventually made a
   book, *The Christian in Industrial Society* (IVP, 1964), the group
   turned out to consist almost entirely of old CICCU men then in
   industry. His subsequent books, particularly *The Christian Citizen*
   (Hodder and Stoughton, 1969), also contributed substantially to
   the whole discussion in a constructive and biblical way.

Chapter 8
63 The moving spirit behind this was Bishop Stephen Neill, who
   was then Chaplain of Trinity College. He had been, in turn, on
   both the CICCU and SCM committees in the 1920s and, though
   he was very much in sympathy with the CICCU's theology, he
   could never quite appreciate the need for the distinctive witness
   of the CICCU.

64 The first edition of *Basic Christianity* (IVP, 1958) was longer and
   more solid than the revised edition (IVP, 1971). By 1977 it had
   been translated into twenty-six languages and sold over a quarter
   of a million copies in its English editions. IVP reports that it is
   still, of all the evangelistic books that they publish, the one that
   most frequently brings letters telling of conversions through its
   means.

65 Almost every College had on its staff both a Dean of Chapel (often a theologian of ability with teaching and other responsibilities) and a Chaplain, who was a younger ordained man entrusted with the welfare of students and pastoral functions. Some Colleges had more than one Chaplain. Inevitably the Chaplains liked to spend time with the CICCU members and sought to have some influence in areas where they thought the CICCU needed help. At this time most Chaplains were somewhat liberal High-Churchmen; only two or three were evangelical.

66 Basil F. C. Atkinson, *Basil's Recollections* (1966).

Chapter 9

67 These letters were reprinted as a pamphlet and published by *The Times* under the title *Fundamentalism: A Religious Problem* (Times Publishing Co., 1955).

68 The article was in *The Bishopric* of February 1965, pp. 24–26. To quote more fully: 'It offers authority and security, quick and sure, to a generation restless and insecure. Other and more wholesome versions of Christianity offer security indeed – but rather more slowly: the security of growing gradually into the spiritual life of the Church, or the security of bringing a thoughtful and honest mind to rest upon the verities of the Christian faith. But here is security – in a single night. Hither, young man: drown your worries in the rapture of conversion: stifle your doubts by abdicating the use of your mind. A rousing sermon, a hurricane of emotion, a will to leap in the dark – and peace at once and for ever. . . . He (Billy Graham) has gone. Our English fundamentalism remains. It is *heretical*, in one of the classic meanings of heresy, in that it represents a fixation of distorted elements from the Bible without the balanced tradition of scriptural truth as a whole. It is *sectarian*, in that the ardent fundamentalist has no regard for religion outside his own experience and vocabulary. . . . It is time that there was more perception of our true Anglican vocation in theology – to follow the "threefold cord" of Scripture, Tradition and Reason and to withstand the bibliolatrists as stoutly as Hooker withstood the Puritans of his day.

'For the evangelist, there is no golden key. It must be a simple gospel, without sophistication. It must be a gospel which speaks of sin and judgment, with a call for decision. But it must present Christ Himself and not a theory about Him which His apostles did not really teach; and Christ as present in the Sacraments wherein His touch still has its power. It must evoke the response not only of the will and the emotions, but also of the mind. The convert is not called upon to be an "intellectual": he is called upon not to stifle his mind but to allow Christ to open it to a new service of God and his fellows. The Church must pray that men will be raised up with the power so to preach, that the stream of conversions will not be followed by a backwash of moral casualties and disillusioned sceptics.'

69 Some people think that the title 'High-Church' refers to a man's status in the Church of England! That is totally wrong. The High-Church tradition in the nineteenth century was proud to take a 'high' view of the Church of England and its sacraments, as opposed to the Low-Church (mainly, but by no means entirely, evangelical) and the Broad-Church (moderate) emphases. Some older High-Church leaders were practically Lutheran and had much in common with evangelicals on the essentials, often standing together against the Broad-Church party. But as the nineteenth century progresssed the High-Church party became increasingly influenced by Roman Catholic theology. Some of this group, often called Anglo-Catholics, accepted the whole (or almost the whole) of Roman theology except the authority of the Pope. By 1900 most of them were also more or less influenced by a liberal attitude to the Bible and so fell back on church tradition (and to some extent reason) as a basis for the faith. By the 1950s the normal High-Church approach was, as Bishop Ramsey put it in his article in *The Bishopric*, an appeal to 'follow the "threefold cord" of Scripture, Tradition and Reason' in which Reason (note the capital letters) had increasingly the final word. Most believed that you became a Christian by baptism and grew up as a Christian by attendance at Communion and the other ritual ordinances of the church. Ramsey typically disliked (see quote in note 68 above) any idea of abrupt conversion and wanted people to grow 'gradually into the spiritual life of the Church'. The opposition to evangelical teaching was therefore based broadly on a very different view of Christian truth and life. The situation in the High-Church party, however, became rather fluid and the views which had been characteristic earlier (*e.g.* their attitude to baptism) are not always so strongly held today.

70 *York Journal of Convocation*, May 1957, pp. 92f. The theological position of the speaker may be judged by the fact that he ended his

speech by saying: 'I do not think there will ever be a revival of great religion until there has been a revival of great poetry'! He was seconding a resolution to receive a report on education which included a jumble of accusations about 'uncritical fundamentalism' as 'sponsored in general by the Inter-Varsity Fellowship and by the Christian Unions'. Among 'characteristic views' were listed such a view of the church as led 'even to the extent of boycotting the college chapel; a radical view of the penal atonement, together with a rejection of baptismal regeneration and indifference to Holy Communion; intolerant individualism; a negative attitude to morals (*sic*) . . . ' (Perhaps the last phrase was meant to refer to social ethics, but since it was general it was taken to be more sinister in its implications.) Even at the time of the controversy it was hard to take some of these points very seriously. In retrospect, now that few liberals are so wedded to the church as an institution, or to College Chapel, or to baptismal regeneration, or to strictly New Testament ethics, the criticism seems rather wide of the mark.

71 In 1962 the SCM Press published *A Survey of Christianity in the Universities*, based on figures for 1961-2. By then the Cambridge Methodist Society membership was down to 300 and the total national membership of Methodist societies was 2,000. Membership of the eighteen Baptist societies was 650 and the eighteen Congregational and Presbyterian societies 350. This survey gives IVF membership as 3,000 in the Universities, and SCM 3,700, including 400 in Cambridge. In the 1940s the Methodist Society in Cambridge had claimed to have nearly 1,000 members.

72 Before the Second World War the more strongly reformed independent churches and the Pentecostal churches tended not to encourage their young people to go to Universities. If they did go it was usually to a local University and not to Oxford or Cambridge.

73 The smaller College groups with no strong prayer fellowship of their own had been the backbone of the DPM in this lean time. They valued it as some of the larger groups did not.

Acknowledgments

This book cannot pretend to be a piece of thorough research. It depends heavily on secondary sources and in particular on J. C. Pollock's *A Cambridge Movement*. The author is deeply indebted to Mr Pollock for his permission to quote extensively from that book. To the wide-ranging research that Mr Pollock has done I have added in certain areas only. My conclusions are not always identical with his, but anyone who reads both books will quickly see that in some chapters I rely on his work very extensively.

The author's only claim to be able to write such a history is that, although he is not a historian, he has had a fairly unique contact with the CICCU over a considerable slice of its history. His father and mother and their brothers and other friends were all involved in their time (1876–1905). He has known personally a representative group of those who were leaders in the CICCU since 1895 and he himself had the privilege of being up from 1938 to 1945. He has also had fairly continuous involvement with the CICCU ever since. He therefore has to acknowledge his debt to a large number of former CICCU members of all generations who have talked about their time in Cambridge and have sometimes shown him documents from the time that they were students.

A number of people have read parts of the manuscript in draft and made invaluable comments. My wife tackled the most difficult task of all, which was to transcribe my original manuscript into legible type, and without her help it would have been very difficult to finish the job. So many people have given information, advice and criticism that I cannot list them all.

Finally the author must acknowledge his debt to the contemporaries who constituted the CICCU of his day. Like everyone else who has been caught up in its life, he must confess how much he owes to its ongoing influence. To write this history has been a fresh reminder of how much we have all owed to that group of raw but spiritually privileged fellow-students, mostly a year or so older than ourselves, who set an example and gave us a vision for Christian living and Christian witness in Cambridge. That is to say, we all have to confess how much we owe to a remarkable work of God in the lives of men and women and to those friends who demonstrated it.

Chief sources

A. There are two major sources that cover much of the ground up to 1910 and 1952 respectively. Most of the quotations for which no other reference is given come from Pollock.

Tissington Tatlow, *The Story of the Student Christian Movement of Great Britain and Ireland* (SCM, 1933).

J. C. Pollock, *A Cambridge Movement* (John Murray, 1953).

B. Other printed books and pamphlets:

G. R. Balleine, *A History of the Evangelical Party in the Church of England* (Longmans Green, 1908).

B. Godfrey Buxton, *The Reward of Faith in the Life of Barclay Fowell Buxton 1860–1946* (Lutterworth, 1949).

F. D. Coggan (ed.), *Christ and the Colleges. A History of the Inter-Varsity Fellowship of Evangelical Unions* (IVFEU, 1934).

W. H. T. Gairdner, *D. M. Thornton. A Study in Missionary Ideals and Methods* (Hodder and Stoughton, 1908).

Norman P. Grubb, *C. T. Studd: Cricketer and Pioneer* (Lutterworth, 1933).

C. F. Harford-Battersby, *Pilkington of Uganda* (Marshall Brothers, no date).

Marcus L. Loane, *Archbishop Mowll. The Biography of H. W. K. Mowll* (Hodder and Stoughton, 1960).

Basil Matthews, *John R. Mott, World Citizen* (SCM, 1934).

Handley C. G. Moule, *Charles Simeon* (1892; reissued IVF, 1948).

Handley C. G. Moule, *Thoughts on Christian Sanctity* (Seeley, 1885).

C. Padwick, *Temple Gairdner of Cairo* (SPCK, 1929).

J. C. Pollock, *The Cambridge Seven* (IVF, 1955).

E. Porter, *Victorian Cambridge* (Dennis Dobson, 1969).

Ruth Rouse, *The World Student Christian Federation* (SCM, 1948).

Eugene Stock, *The History of the Church Missionary Society*, vols. I–III (CMS, 1899).

Oliver Tomkins, *The Life of Edward Woods* (SCM, 1957).

Max Warren, *Crowded Canvas: Some Experiences of a Lifetime* (Hodder and Stoughton, 1974).

Robert P. Wilder, *The Great Commission* (Oliphants, 1936).

Robert P. Wilder, *The Student Volunteer Movement* (SVM, New York, 1938).

E. S. Woods and F. B. MacNutt, *Theodore, Bishop of Winchester. A Memoir of Frank Theodore Woods 1874–1932* (SPCK, 1933).

A Brief History of the Inter-Varsity Fellowship of Evangelical Christian Unions (IVFECU, *c.* 1928).

Fundamentalism: A Religious Problem. Letters to the Editor of The Times *and a Leading Article* (Times Publishing Co., 1955).

Old Paths in Perilous Times (First ed., Marshall, Morgan and Scott, 1913; Second ed., IVF, *c.* 1932).

C. Other sources not detailed in the Notes:

CICCU records.

The personal diaries of David B. Barclay for 1897, 1898, 1899.

Dr Basil Atkinson's handwritten memorandum entitled *Basil's Recollections*. About four copies were made and one is in the UCCF Office.

Cambridge University Missionary Band prayer letters.

Personal discussions and correspondence, some of it tape-recorded, with Godfrey Buxton, Joe Church, Norman Grubb, Kenneth Hooker, Noel Palmer and a number of others.

Written memoranda by a considerable number of CICCU leaders for the period 1953–73.

Mr Ben Harder, at the time a research student at Aberdeen and now Professor of Church History in the Graduate Department of Winnipeg Bible College, Canada, provided me with a number of scripts of interviews and copies of material from the SCM archives. He had obtained these in connection with his own researches on the period up to 1910.

J. C. Pollock, *A Cambridge Movement*, gives further extensive references, some of which have been consulted.

Index